P9-CFE-525

Which
Ad
Pulled
Best?

Eighth Edition

Which Ad Pulled Best?

50 Case Histories on
How to Write and Design Ads That Work

Philip Ward Burton
Indiana University

Scott C. Purvis
President, Gallup & Robinson, Inc.

NTC Business Books
NTC/Contemporary Publishing Group

Library of Congress Cataloging-in-Publication Data

Which ad pulled best? / [edited by] Philip Ward Burton, Scott C.
    Purvis. — 8th ed.
        p.   cm.
    ISBN 0-8442-3514-8
    1. Advertising.   2. Copy advertising—Evaluation.   I. Burton,
Philip Ward.   II. Purvis, Scott C.
HF5823.W467   1992
659.1—dc20   92-29612
                                                        CIP

Published by NTC Business Books, a division of NTC Publishing Group.
© 1996 by NTC Publishing Group, 4255 West Touhy Avenue,
Lincolnwood (Chicago), Illinois 60646-1975 U.S.A.
All rights reserved. No part of this book may be reproduced, stored
in a retrieval system, or transmitted in any form or by any means,
electronic, mechanical, photocopying, recording or otherwise, without
the prior permission of NTC Publishing Group.
Library of Congress Catalog Card Number 89-64281
Manufactured in the United States of America.

90 VL 9 8 7 6 5 4 3

Contents

Foreword

What kinds of advertising copy and illustrations get the best results? Whether you're a practitioner or a student of advertising and marketing, you'll have opinions based upon experience, common sense, intuition, and sheer guesswork. Sometimes these opinions help, and sometimes they don't.

To help you in creative evaluation, this book shows you, through tested advertisements, what elements were responsible for their performance. When you see in example after example that certain principles work most of the time, you will begin to rely less on guesswork and intuition and more on these guiding doctrines. You'll learn some of the success factors that increase the pulling power of advertisements. You'll see advertising techniques that attract attention, create interest, arouse desire, and stimulate action.

Philip Ward Burton, professor in the School of Journalism, Indiana University, edited this new edition and wrote all the critical analyses in the accompanying *Instructor's Manual.* Professor Burton is ideally qualified for this work through his years of experience as a practitioner and as an outstanding educator.

Besides providing all-new advertisements for this eighth edition, Scott Purvis freely shared with us the Gallup & Robinson evaluation techniques so widely used in the industry. Interviews with some of advertising's top practitioners were also contributed by Mr. Purvis.

We're grateful, too, for the contributions of Readex examples by Richard L. Rogers, Sr., EVP/ Corporate Development of Readex, Inc.

The eighth edition of this popular book fits admirably into the list of books we offer practitioners, teachers, and students of advertising. Most of all, it brings real-life experiences to the classroom.

The Editors
NTC Business Books

The authors wish to thank William H. Van Pelt, Jr. for his contribution to this book.

Consumer Advertisements Tested by Gallup & Robinson

EXAMPLE	11	12	13	14	15
Page	63	65	67	69	71
Advertiser(s)	J & J Purpose L'Oreal	Sears K-Mart	Ray-o-vac Energizer	Shout All	Safeguard Dove
Product or Service	Skin care	Clothing	Batteries	Detergent	Soap
Publication(s) Used	*Self* *Ladies' Home Journal*	*Ladies' Home Journal*	*People* *Time*	*Ladies' Home Journal* *Good Housekeeping*	*People* *Ladies' Home Journal*
Problems/Principles Demonstrated	Question headlines News/benefit headlines Identification techniques Insets as attention-getters Illustrations with dominant elements Linkage of headline and copy	Misleading headlines Linkage of headline and opening copy Dominant element illustrations Importance of product focus	Starter words for headlines Advertisements without headlines Dominant element illustrations Pulling power of coupons Advertisements with no focal center Benefit headlines Importance of achieving advertiser identification Numbers in headlines for pulling power	Performance of product sold Copy approaches to be used Problem-solution approach Before and after illustrations Unusual vs. stereotyped illustrations Finding the right appeal News/benefit headlines Advertiser identification techniques	Selecting the suitable approach Picture-caption creative technique Advertisements without headlines Endorsements by doctors Unifying advertisements by closely relating headline, illustration, and opening copy Advertisements that can be understood at a glance Cartoon strips as an advertising device

EXAMPLE	16	17	18	19	20
Page	73	75	77	79	81
Advertiser(s)	Isuzu	General Foods	Pontiac Chrysler	Kretschmer	Kikkoman Tabasco
Product or Service	Autos (trucks and vans)	International coffee	Autos	Wheat germ	Sauce
Publication(s) Used	*Sports Illustrated*	*People* *Cosmopolitan*	*Sports Illustrated*	*Bon Appétit* *Better Homes and Gardens*	*Life* *Ladies' Home Journal*
Problems/Principles Demonstrated	Novelty approach in headlines and illustrations Whimsy in advertising Bold illustration approach Headlines without benefit Techniques for achieving strong identification Humor as an advertising tool Tying headlines with illustrations	Misleading copy approach Appetite appeal in food advertisements Cleverness in illustrations Use of "borrowed interest" Power of the word "new" Combining headlines and illustrations to make clear what is being advertised Ways to create strong advertiser identification Stressing products with current appeal	Stereotyped illustrations Headlines without benefit Power of comparison tables Use of endorsements Identification of advertisers Use of reverse type	Coupons as reader attraction Humor in advertisements Headlines without benefit Product-in-use illustrations Breaking the "rules" in designing advertisements	Overshadowing the product with competing interest Elements causing weak identification Elements resulting in strong identification Headlines weakened by distracting elements Value to advertisement of presenting something new

EXAMPLE	21	22	23	24	25
Page	83	85	87	89	91
Advertiser(s)	General Electric Motorola	Colgate	Quaker Oats	Goodyear Pirelli	Lipton Tetley
Product or Service	Cellular phones	Toothbush	Cookies	Tires	Tea
Publication(s) Used	*Business Week*	*People* *Ladies' Home Journal*	*Ladies' Home Journal*	*Time* *Newsweek*	*Better Homes and Gardens*
Problems/Principles Demonstrated	Offbeat illustrations Use of a celebrity Testimonial that lacks credibility Close tie-in of headline and illustration	Use of demonstration in illustration Dominant element illustrations Eye flow in illustrations Value of close tie-in of illustration, headline, and opening copy Headlines that can be understood quickly	Effect of recipes on advertising readership Need for appetite appeal in food advertisements Tie-in of promotions for two products Advantage of advertising a popular product People vs. things in advertising Strong identification as an aid to memorability	Use of label headlines Unconventional placement of logos Effect of reverse type Typography that uses curved lines Putting the name of the advertiser in headline for identification Enhancing product focus through use of color	Sensory words in food copy Need for appetite appeal in food advertisements Copy that uses a play on words in headlines Need for clarity in headlines

EXAMPLE	26	27	28	29	30
Page	93	95	97	99	101
Advertiser(s)	Sony Panasonic	Purina Reward	Braun Norelco	Kraft	Kitchen Aid Jenn-Air
Product or Service	Cordless phones	Dog food	Shavers	Salad dressing	Cooktops
Publication(s) Used	*Bon Appétit* *Glamour*	*People*	*U.S. News and World Report*	*Ladies' Home Journal* *People*	*Better Homes and Gardens* *Bon Appétit*
Problems/Principles Demonstrated	Headlines without benefit Numbers in headlines Enhancing identification by using advertiser's name in headlines Showing the product in use Effect of reverse type	Celebrities in illustrations Headlines without benefit Humor as a negative element Ingredient comparison as a creative tool Strong identification for memorability	Intruding layout elements into the copy Headlines with strong impact in content and appearance Photography vs. artwork in demonstrating a product	Using ''new'' in headlines Identifying the product or advertiser in headlines Symbolic layout devices as an aid to memory Effect of reverse type Using the headline, illustration, and logo for strong identification Color as an aid for attention and product selling Effectiveness of question headline	Showing the product in use News-type headlines Intruding layout elements into the copy Use of captions for increasing interest, readership, and understanding Effect of color contrast

EXAMPLE	31	32	33	34	35
Page	103	105	107	109	111
Advertiser(s)	Asics Nike	Jello	Panasonic Sony	Canon UC1 Panasonic Palmcorder	Quaker
Product or Service	Athletic shoes	Gelatin Pudding snacks	Camcorders	Camcorders	Instant oatmeal
Publication(s) Used	*Sports Illustrated*	*Ladies' Home Journal* *Better Homes and Gardens*	*People* *U.S. News and World Report*	*People*	*Good Housekeeping* *People*
Problems/Principles Demonstrated	Delayed answers to question headlines Focusing on the product in the illustration Use of long copy Headlines without benefit Extra large type for attention-getting headlines	Recipes in food advertisements Headlines without benefit Readership fall-off because of reverse type "Giantism" in illustrations Food advertisements and appetite appeal Seasonal tie-ins in advertisements	Need for quick understanding of an advertisement Direct vs. indirect headlines Focusing on the product by placing it near focal center Need for long copy in selling complex products Human interest vs. informative approach	Importance of making the product the "hero" Sentiment vs. information in selling a product Devices to increase identification Illustrations that show the end result of using a product The people vs. things question Designing advertisements to convey message for quick, careless readers	Power of celebrity spokesperson Sentiment as a sales approach Product emphasis techniques Achieving strong identification

EXAMPLE	36	37	38	39	40
Page	113	115	117	119	121
Advertiser(s)	Hyundai Nissan	La-Z-Boy Sleeper Grange	National Hertz	Pioneer Panasonic	Panasonic Bose
Product or Service	Autos	Furniture	Rental Cars	Laser disc players	VCR programming Home theater system
Publication(s) Used	*Time* *Newsweek*	*Metropolitan Home* *People*	*Time* *Forbes*	*Playboy*	*People*
Problems/Principles Demonstrated	Headlines suffering from "sameness" Illustration stereotypes Comparison copy as a reader attraction Use of prices to spur interest Names in headlines to enhance identification	Product-in-use illustrations Use of product name in headline Advertisements without headlines Importance of product focus	Advertisements without headlines Designing advertisements for quick product recognition Competitive advantage of well-known name	Benefit headlines vs. headlines without benefit Illustration of product Elements contributing to strong identification Effect on readership of play-on-word headlines How to ensure quick registration of copy message Emphasizing product details over people in advertising new, expensive, and technical items	Strength of news-benefit headlines Use of take-out (call-out) lines to guide readers Technique for focusing on the product Cleverness vs. clarity in headlines Including elements that result in strong identification Tie-in of headline, illustration, and opening copy

Business Advertisements Tested by Readex

EXAMPLE	41	42	43	44	45
Page	125	127	129	131	133
Advertiser(s)	Alcoa	ProPlus	Devoe	Beefmasters Breeders Universal (BBU)	McDonald's
Product or Service	Aluminum	Isolated soy protein	Paint	Heifer replacement	Fast food
Publication(s) Used	*Ward's Auto World*	*School Foodservice & Nutrition*	*The Paint Dealer*	*Progressive Farmer*	*Journal of the American Dietetic Association*
Problems/Principles Demonstrated	Advantage achieved through product display in illustration	Real-life situations for reader involvement in illustrations	Use of subheads	Risks in using testimonials	Use of label headlines
	Manufacturer-oriented copy vs. reader-oriented copy	Use of unusual words in headlines to catch attention	Direct benefit advertising vs. institutional advertising for business readers	Products vs. people in illustrations	Dominant element principle in illustrations
	Use of subheads to lead readers through the copy	Importance of finding a copy appeal that will attract a wide audience	Importance of having people to whom readers can relate in illustrations	Advertisements without headlines	Questionable typography
					Directing copy to professional audience

EXAMPLE	46	47	48	49	50
Page	135	137	139	141	143
Advertiser(s)	Falcon Systems	Shell	Malvern Instruments	Parker	Spacesaver
Product or Service	Silicon graphics	Rotella oil	Particle sizing	Refrigeration controls	Storage systems
Publication(s) Used	*Computer Graphics World*	*Fleet Owner*	*Powder and Bulk Engineering*	*The News: Airconditioning, Heating & Refrigeration*	*Architecture*
Problems/Principles Demonstrated	Matching copy to the needs of the audience	Using name of product in headline	Problem-solution technique in business advertising	Achieving understanding by tie-in of headline, illustrations, subhead, and opening copy	Symbolism as a layout device
	Interesting headlines vs. label headlines	Strong use of testimonials	Use of "borrowed interest" to attract readers	Intruding layout elements into copy space	Failure to ensure quick registration of ad message
	Need of technically minded readers for useful information	Using graphics to demonstrate product benefits	Power through use of large type in headlines	Using numbers in headlines	Effect of reverse type
	Use of advertisements as catalog pages in business publications			Headlines that require mental effort	

Principles Demonstrated
by Tested Advertisements

List of Advertisers

*Example number(s) in **boldface**.

The Who-What-How of Testing Printed Advertising

Two prominent research organizations tested the fifty pairs of advertisements you will find in this book—Gallup & Robinson and Readex. The former tested the forty consumer advertisements; the latter, the ten business advertisements.

In the following material you will learn the methodology employed by these two organizations. Next, you will learn the research techniques used by the Starch advertisement readership service, another well-known research organization. In addition, there will be a general discussion of research, various methodologies, criticisms and virtues, and, finally, guidelines to advertisers that stem from research findings.

ADVERTISING RESEARCH IS A RELATIVE NEWCOMER

In the early days of advertising there was almost no research—keeping records of inquiries produced by advertisements was about it. Then came the depression, when cost-conscious advertisers demanded to know the factors behind the success or failure of advertisements. Thus, you might say that meaningful scientific research began in the 1930s.

Advertising research has been controversial from the start. It is *still* the subject of debate among advertisers, advertising agency people, and researchers themselves; there is no system on which all agree. Still, much of the guesswork of early advertisers has been eliminated. From research, we now have guidelines that, if followed, give advertisers much more assurance of obtaining good readership, inquiries, or sales.

GALLUP & ROBINSON METHODOLOGY

Gallup & Robinson has pioneered a variety of systems to help advertisers and agencies evaluate the effectiveness of their advertising in the marketplace and gain a better understanding of the advertising process. The systems have been used to evaluate over 120,000 print ads and 60,000 television commercials.

The examples that are used in this book were tested under Gallup & Robinson's Magazine Impact Research Service (MIRS). Its specific objectives are to (1) assess in-market performance of individual ads; (2) analyze overall advertising campaign and strategy effectiveness relative to previous history and the performance of the competition; and (3) identify and evaluate the effectiveness of competitive selling propositions and executional approaches within specific industries or product categories.

To accomplish its objectives, the MIRS system permits users to assess their own and competitive advertising appearing in regularly scheduled test issues of major consumer, news, and women's service magazines. The sample size for each survey is approximately 150 men and/or women, ages eighteen and older. Qualified readers are located by continuous household canvass in ten metropolitan areas geographically dispersed across the United States. Respondents qualify by having read two of the last four issues of the test magazine or others in the same classification, but they must not have read the current issue.

The test magazine is placed in the respondent's home, and the respondent is interviewed by telephone the following day. Readers are given no advance information of the nature of the interview but are requested to read the magazine on the day of placement and not to read it on the day of the interview.

During the telephone interview, respondents are asked preliminary questions to determine readership. A list of ads appearing in the magazine is read, and respondents are asked which ads they remember. For each ad the respondent claims to recall, the following Impact questions are asked.

1. You may be familiar with other ads for _____, but thinking only of this issue, please describe the ad as you remember it. What did the ad look like and say?

2. What sales points or arguments for buying did they show or talk about?

3. What did you learn about the (product/service) from this ad?

4. What thoughts and feelings went through your mind when you looked at the ad?

5. The advertiser tried to increase your interest in his (product/service). How was your buying interest affected?

- Increased considerably
- Increased somewhat
- Not affected
- Decreased somewhat
- Decreased considerably

6. What was in the ad that makes you say that?

7. What brand of this type of product did you buy last (or what company's service did you last use)?

Each interview concludes with a series of classification questions.

The Impact questions yield a rich quality of verbatim testimony that is used to produce three basic measurements of advertising effectiveness.

1. *Intrusiveness (Proved Name Registration)*—the percentage of respondents who can accurately describe the ad the day following exposure. This measure is an indicator of the ad's ability to command attention. For comparative purposes, percentages are adjusted for space/color unit cost and issue level.

2. *Idea communication*—the distribution of respondents' descriptions of the ad's selling propositions and of their reactions to the ad. This measure is an indicator of what ideas and feelings are communicated by the ad.

3. *Persuasion (Favorable Buying Attitude)*—the distribution of respondent statements of how the ad affected purchase interest. This measure is a relative indicator of the ad's ability to persuade. For corporate advertising, the persuasion measure indicates the extent to which the ad made a strong case for the advertiser.

Because different product categories have different interest levels, the norms of performance can vary by category. For this reason, Gallup & Robinson uses category-specific norms. The extensive coverage of MIRS provides a wide range of sex-specific, normative data for most product groups.

Each Ad Impact report on client and/or competitive advertisements contains the following:

- Pictorial roster for all ads tested
- Intrusiveness (Proved Name Registration) measure
- Idea Communication profile
- Persuasion (Favorable Buying Attitude) measure
- Norms
- Verbatim testimony for the ad
- Sample characteristics

MIRS also allows for testing an ad that is not published in a MIRS schedule magazine. The advertiser may tip into a test issue so that the test ad appears as if it ran naturally. The technique is useful for pretesting an ad or for providing extra posttest opportunities (for example, to obtain a full sample test on regional runs).

In addition to diagnostic information that explains how performance can be improved, the MIRS system yields evaluative measures of intrusiveness and persuasion. Intrusiveness is measured by Proved Name Registration (PNR) and is the ability of the ad to stop and hold the audience's attention to the advertiser's name. Persuasion is measured by Favorable Buying Attitude (FBA) and is the ability of the ad to increase buying interest or generate favor for the product, service, or idea. It is important to note that Intrusiveness and Persuasion are not correlated at any time.

READEX READER INTEREST STUDIES

Readex, an independent mail survey research firm, has been designing and conducting readership research for print communications since 1947. The firm conducts about 400 studies per year for over 240 different publications.

Readex offers three off-the-shelf readership studies: Red Sticker II™, MESSAGE IMPACT®, and Ad Perception™.

Red Sticker II is closest to a "classical" ad readership study. It provides measurement of both ads and editorial. This study asks readers three questions of each item studied: Did you see it? Did you read it? Did you find it of interest? "Interest" in advertising is considered, by Readex, to be a fundamental element in the selling process. The firm says that to sell a product or service a prospective customer must first be made aware of the opportunity (seeing), and sufficient interest must then be developed (reading) to motivate the prospect toward the sale. "Interest" equals a considered opinion of the material seen and read.

MESSAGE IMPACT is a more in-depth study that combines qualitative and quantitative readership dimensions. This study type is designed to answer the questions most often asked by advertisers and agencies.

- Ratings for an ad's stopping power are calculated. Readers are asked to rate an ad on attention-getting ability, believability, and information value.

- Readers are asked to list actions taken or planned as a result of seeing the ad or offer feedback on their impressions of a company's image.

- A transcript of verbatim comments is provided, including comments on the ad's message, the feeling the reader received from the advertisement, or the reader's perceived image of the company.

Ad Perception provides quantitative feedback on the three basic elements of effective ads. Readers evaluate each ad by indicating whether or not the ad was attention-getting, believable, and informative. The attention-getting score refers to the visual stopping power of the ad. The other two scores (believability and information value) refer to the message found in the copy of the ad. A successful ad is usually believable (credible) as well as informative (in terms of specifications, applications, etc).

Results for each of the above study types are published in readership study reports, usually available three to five weeks after the study closes.

Reports for Red Sticker II and Ad Perception are broken into several sections. First is information on the Purpose and Method. This is followed by a Traffic Flow chart, a list of high scoring ads, scores for size/color categories, scores for product/service categories, and graphical presentations of historical averages for both size/color as well as product/service.

For MESSAGE IMPACT, reports have four sections of information: Purpose and Method; Reader Ratings ("this ad" compared to averages for product/service and size/color categories); Reader Actions ("this ad" compared to averages for product/service and size/color categories); and Reader verbatim comments.

Methodology

Readex has chosen to specialize in surveys through the mail. A readership survey mailing usually consists of (1) an Alert letter, (2) a survey kit that includes a cover letter with a questionnaire *or* a duplicate copy of the study issue, plus a business reply envelope, and (3) a reminder mailing. Completed surveys are returned to Readex for processing.

ADVANTAGES OF THE READEX METHODOLOGY

1. Lowest cost per completed interview among all survey methods.

2. Suitable for large samples.

3. Large geographic scope plus geographically representative.

4. Eliminates interviewer bias.

5. Respondents answer at their convenience; allows more time to answer thought provoking or technical questions.

6. Encourages candid responses by assuring anonymity.

ROPER STARCH WORLDWIDE, INC.

For many years the Starch Advertisement Readership Service has been used widely by a variety of advertisers. Because the Starch service uses recognition testing, it is based upon actual behavior. This means that respondents are asked what they actually read in a publication instead of what they "usually" read.

In conducting the research, Starch interviewers first qualify respondents as having read the publication used for test purposes. After this, they check the advertisement reading of the respondents. When all the interviews are completed, the results are totaled and readers are put into one of three categories.

1. *Noted.* These are respondents who have merely remembered seeing the advertisement but can't identify the product or advertiser.

2. *Advertiser-associated.* In this case, the readers have seen the advertisement and have read enough to be able to identify the product and/or advertiser.

3. *Read-most.* Here the readers have read 50 percent or more of the advertisement's reading matter.

As part of the service, Starch provides cost ratios of the advertisements and ranks them in terms of the dollars expended to obtain readers. An advertiser can find out how much it costs to merely get an advertisement seen, seen and associated, or read most. These figures have different meanings for different advertisers. For instance, a soft-drink advertiser who uses little body copy is more interested in advertiser-associated than read-most, but the advertiser of an expensive automobile might want to achieve a high read-most figure.

MOTIVATIONAL RESEARCH

A motivational research study utilizes a series of free-flowing conversations by typical consumers in the course of which they hopefully will express their true feelings about the service or product being investigated. Such a report may describe the kinds of associations engendered. These might be obtained through psychological testing that uses projective techniques such as free word association, sentence completion, or picture responses.

Out of the foregoing will come analyses of what the findings mean to advertisers, because interpretations must be furnished to explain the significance of consumers' stream-of-consciousness conversations or the associations discovered by clinical psychologists administering the tests.

Motivational research investigators usually proceed on the assumption that they do not know what their research may uncover, because irrational behavior, drives, fears, and desires may lie behind people's reactions to the product or situation being studied. Out of the study may come reasons that respondents could give the ordinary researcher, but probably will not.

Most motivational research is concerned with the subconscious level and has been prompted by the feeling that asking people directly how they feel about something will fail to uncover how they *really* feel underneath. Although motivational research—or MR, as it is known—is still practiced, it is no longer the fad it once was when the advertising industry thought it provided a sure formula for creative success.

INQUIRY TESTING

Inquiry tests are made by keeping track of the number of inquiries produced by each advertisement. For example, an advertiser offers something free, or at nominal cost, and then sees how many people are interested enough to follow up on the offer. A second advertisement making the same offer will then be run and resulting inquiries counted. The results from the two advertisements can then be compared on the basis of inquiries produced.

In order to be certain that results come from a specific advertisement, the advertiser inserts a key number in the coupon, or in a paragraph near the bottom of the advertisement in which the offer appears, and suggests that respondents write in to take advantage of the offer. "Keys" take many forms, such as a post office box number, a street address, or a room number in an office building, and can be changed each time a different advertisement is run.

Inquiries are sorted according to the advertisement that produced them as they come in. Records are kept of how many inquiries are produced by each advertisement run in each different publication. Such records show not only which advertisements are producing the most inquiries but which publications as well.

In the case of mail order advertising, a record can also show which inquiries are most valuable in developing sales. When mail order advertisers get an inquiry (say, a request for a catalog), they follow up with literature designed to make a sale. Then, as sales are made, they relate the number and size of orders back to the inquiry and the advertisement that made the first contact. In this way, mail order advertisers keep track not only of which advertisements produce the most inquiries but also which locate the best prospects—quite often there is a difference.

What about non-mail order advertisers? They too can follow up inquiries sparked by advertisements by having salespeople call. Brokerage houses and insurance companies have successfully used follow-up systems to determine the quality of inquiries, as have direct selling organizations, whose salespeople call directly on homes when following up inquiries produced by advertisements for vacuum cleaners, sewing machines, baby equipment, and similar products and services.

Although sales don't necessarily match inquiry returns, such returns are generally a good indication of the interest developed by a given advertisement. Comparisons of inquiries produced by different advertisements also indicate the relative interest created by each. This is especially true if some qualifying device is used in an advertisement, such as requiring people asking for the booklet, sample, or whatever to pay out some amount—anywhere from a few cents to several dollars—in order to obtain the offer. Such a requirement tends to discourage those not truly interested.

An advertisement itself can be a qualifying device.

If it delves deeply into the subject of the merchandise for sale, it is likely that only firm prospects will read the whole advertisement down to the point where the offer is made. Then there are those advertisements that contain "buried" offers, the kind made in the middle of the body text. In this case, no coupon will be included in the advertisement.

SALES TESTS

For many advertisers, especially those in the mail order business, sales rather than mere inquiries provide the real test of effectiveness. Book publishers in particular find it profitable to sell directly through published advertising, and many products elicit sales directly through long television commercials. Here again, advertisers use keys to determine the advertisements producing the most sales and the publications that are the best result getters.

Once an advertisement has proved to be a big sales producer, it may be run over and over again without change. It may, however, be tested against a new advertisement to be certain that its sales power isn't falling off.

COPY TESTING IS NOT INFALLIBLE

Errors occur frequently in copy testing because there are so many variables that throw off results. Here are some possible problems affecting test validity.

1. Differences in the publications used.

2. Differences in page locations in the publications used (despite some experts' claims that page location is unimportant).

3. Variations in reading habits, inquiry mood, and buying activity at different times of the year.

4. Natural variations resulting simply from the law of averages.

5. Differences in the general interest in the product or service offered. This can well be the most important of the foregoing variables. Furthermore, product interest may vary among different products in a line or for the same products at different times of the year.

If all of these factors are present in a copy test, results can differ widely without the copy being changed. Thus, the more these factors are kept constant between two advertisements, the more valid the comparison. Eliminating variables from copy tests is almost impossible—no matter how ingenious the testing method, some variance always seems to show up.

This is true even in the most rigidly controlled split run offered by large-circulation publications.

In the split run, one advertisement is placed in half the copies printed in a particular issue and another advertisement in the other half. Some publications make this split every other copy coming off the press; then, when that issue is distributed, there is a 50-50 chance that the two different advertisements will be distributed to equal audiences.

GUIDELINES FOR COPY REVEALED BY COPY TESTING

As you will hear over and over again, no single formula works successfully all the time in creating advertisements. Testing simply gives rise to general conclusions—it indicates what is most *likely* to work. If heeded by the person writing copy, the principles stemming from generalities may result in techniques and approaches that will be more right than wrong.

Following are some of the guidelines suggested by copy testing.

1. *Offer a major benefit.* Benefits take different forms—a product most people want; a product easy to get; a product worth paying for; a product priced as low as possible.

2. *Make it easy to see and read.* Despite all the findings of copy testing, this advice is frequently ignored, even by the most sophisticated advertisers and advertising agencies. Picture the benefit clearly, simply, and as large as possible. It should be presented with easy-to-grasp language—simple, convincing prose supported by a layout that ties in and is equally easy to follow.

3. *Establish audience identity.* Make it easy for viewers to see themselves in pictures on the screen or in illustrations in the publication. The copy, too, should involve the audience by giving ideas on how to use or profit from the benefit. In short, establish a relationship between the audience and the benefit.

4. *Attract by being new.* Advertising's strongest weapon is news—new products, new uses for products, new benefits. Accordingly, the most powerful advertisements include something novel in the benefit that offers new reasons to buy. To do this, successful advertisements fit the news approach by using action pictures, modern settings, active language written in present tense, and word pictures.

5. *Be believable.* Sadly enough, when different vocations are rated according to honesty and credibility,

advertising people are rated near or at the bottom. Brag and boast copy and extravagant and slick copywriter phrases are primarily responsible for this perception. To achieve believability, don't make unreasonable claims. Avoid the blue-sky approach in describing benefits. Supply proof for claims. In pictures and illustrations, show the product realistically; don't doctor it so that there is a difference between the product in the advertising and that in the hand. This same observation also holds for what you say in the copy.

6. *Stress what is unique.* Advertising people express uniqueness as a ''point of difference'' or ''USP''—unique selling proposition. Both terms refer to an attractive feature available solely in the advertised product and promoted as an exclusive benefit. The difference could be in styling, price, size, or ease of use. Any experienced copywriter, when asked to write about a product or service, will ask: ''What's different about it?'' That is the starting point of the creative process.

What you have read in the foregoing only touches upon the generalities stemming from copy research. Still, all six of these points are important and, if followed, will help you avoid some of the most common mistakes in writing copy.

Analysis of *Which Ad Pulled Best?* Examples Reveal Six Ways to Make Advertisements Pull Better

The more impressive the benefit, the greater the result in advertising. That is the one conclusion that stands out in this analysis of advertisements compared in the *Which Ad Pulled Best?* examples. Whatever the example, the difference in the way people react to the advertisements can be traced back to the benefit: its believability, and how important it was to the people who read the advertisements.

It takes insight, of course, to determine the key benefits of a product. It may require systematic testing or the more hazardous trial and error of years of experience to narrow the possible benefits down to the one that's a winner. Furthermore, it takes skill to transmit the benefit idea through all the media and techniques of mass communication.

When benefits are presented in the following ways, advertisements will, in general, produce better results.

1. Name the benefit. Be specific about it.

The more specific advertisements are the more successful ones. This holds true regardless of the type of publication, audience, or product. As an example, an advertisement headlined *Low-cost steam—Shop assembled and ready to use* pulled 100 percent more readership than *Steam That Satisfies*.

Similarly, of two advertisements illustrating the same foldaway table for stores, the advertisement headlined *Move up to $100 in iced watermelons in 8 sq. ft. of space* sold 3½ times as much merchandise as the one headlined *8 square feet of dynamic display*.

An offer for a recipe book that included a detailed table of contents drew 136 percent more returns than the offer that merely announced 64 pages packed with methods, recipes, and tips on freezing and canning.

Of two advertisements run under the heading *Relax in Daks*, the one in which the body copy described these slacks most specifically with "No belt, no pressure around the middle. Hidden sponge rubber pads keep a polite but firm grip on your shirt" produced six times as many inquiries as the vaguer "They're self-supporting, shirt-controlling, and leave the body perfectly free."

For a self-sealing envelope, the U.S. Envelope Company tested eight different headlines. Some of the approaches were *So sanitary; Novel; Different; Better; Humid weather never affects.* However, by far, the most successful headline read *Avoid licking glue,* which was the most tangible, specific benefit.

One seeming exception to the virtue of being specific was a headline that read *It's amazing! It's sensational! It's exclusive!* This received twice as much response as *How to become a popular dancer overnight.* Although the winning headline consisted of generalities, the advertisement itself contained a specific feature that the other did not—a detailed diagram of one of the basic dance steps.

2. The product is the big benefit. Tell what it will do.

The more successful advertisements lay greater emphasis on the product. Greater product emphasis coincides with greater success. This is demonstrated by the advertisement headlined *How to get good pictures for sure.* In this advertisement was a large illustration of the camera. It received nearly twice as many inquiries as the one with the same headline that pictured an attractive man and woman gazing admiringly at the very small camera in their hands. In the first advertisement, the product was the hero and held center stage.

What is true of art emphasis is also true of headline-idea emphasis. *Amazing new low-priced electric sprayer for home use makes painting easy* sold 66 percent more sprayers than did the more humanly interesting *Now Tom does every home painting job himself*. This is because the first headline focuses on the product.

In another example, the catchy but not readily grasped headline *Cool heads in hot spots won't let you down* lost overwhelmingly to the straightforward *Copper's blue ribbon ventilators for workers' safety, health, comfort, efficiency*. While this headline won't win any writing awards, it does focus unmistakably on the product.

Sometimes other factors may negate somewhat the effect of product emphasis. An example is that of two advertisements for the same manufacturer, one of which was headlined *Thatcher's 98 years of heating experience means greater comfort at lower cost*. A stark, cold feeling was conveyed by illustrations of four different pieces of heating equipment. The headline for the second advertisement was *Indoor weather made-to-order without lifting your finger*. Here were shown a man and woman in an attractively decorated room, along with a subordinate illustration that featured the one piece of heating equipment needed to provide this "indoor weather." This second advertisement, which pulled three times as many responses, is not only more specific and more humanly interesting, but it also gives more evidence of the benefit to be attained by actual use.

Another example of exceptions to emphasis on product is furnished by a pair of advertisements for Koppers BMU. One is a highly technical discussion of the structure and physical properties of the product. The other, more successful, advertisement, while containing the technical information, features a different approach: Under a photograph of a piece of soap, a man's shirt, and a plastic dish is the headline *Make them whiter and brighter with Koppers BMU*.

3. Make it easy for consumers to visualize the benefit. Keep your advertisements simple.

In one respect or another, simpler advertisements are consistently more successful. Example: For advertisers seeking direct replies, advertisements that include a coupon, thus making it easier for consumers to take action, receive a greater response than those without a coupon for reply.

In addition to looking at simplicity as being synonymous with ease, one can consider it an antonym of complexity. In this sense, those advertisements having a single rather than a multiple focus come out ahead. Eastman Kodak, for example, ran an advertisement di-

vided into four sections. The main headline was *See what you can do with your present equipment*. Each of the four sections featured a different company product. Another issue of the same publication presented an Eastman Kodak advertisement headlined *Because photography is accurate to the last detail*. This was illustrated with a group of mechanical drawings. The copy story was "The magic of photography turns hours of costly drafting room time into a minute-quick job of utmost accuracy."

This second advertisement received 25 percent more attention and 125 percent more readership. Why should this be? The first advertisement was dramatic in its layout, but it made the reader decide on which section to direct his or her attention and on which story to concentrate. Although this multiple-interest advertisement attracted largely the same notice, it lagged far behind the readership earned by the advertisement that developed a single, simple story.

Similarly, an advertisement headlined *Great new insurance plan pays hospital, surgical expenses* did not offer as many benefits as the alternative version, *Now great new insurance plan offers you protection for hospital, surgical, and/or doctors' bills and/or lost income*. Yet the former, simpler advertisement pulled twice as many inquiries as the latter advertisement, indicating that it is sometimes a mistake to tell too much.

This principle still holds even in very small advertisements. A small, one-column advertisement illustrated with only a large bottle read *On our anniversary we're offering you Welch's Grape Juice at a new low price*. When, to this single theme, the company added a party flavor—children in the illustration wearing party hats and the headline *We are playing host to the nation on our anniversary with the greatest price reduction in Welch's history*—it lost readership.

Simplicity also results from unity of concept when a single theme is developed in headline, artwork, and copy. Two advertisements run for a perforator by Cummins Business Machines offer examples. One had a charming illustration of a young mother putting a cookie jar high on a shelf, out of the reach of her mischievous-looking, young son. The headline read *Mr. President—remove opportunity before—not after—fraud*. The second advertisement had no true illustration. On a bold background in white letters made of dots, as if done by a perforator, was the headline *You can't erase a hole. These tiny holes can save you from serious loss*.

In the first advertisement the analogy between the kind and thoughtful mother and the kind and thoughtful employers, each looking out for those dependent upon them, is not farfetched. But in the second and far more successful advertisement, no inferences, however apt, have to be drawn between separate concepts—the entire advertisement consists of one simple, clearly developed idea. Also, the language of the first advertisement is less specific—necessarily so, because a detailed discussion of cookie jars would bear little relation to the perforator being advertised. The point is, then, that not only the simplicity of any single concept, but also the relationship between the product and the consumer, makes the benefit evident.

4. Emphasize the benefit as much as possible. Use large space.

Small space advertisements can work very well. Talk to the average copywriter, however, and you'll soon find that he or she prefers to work with larger space units. In the larger space you can tell readers more about what the product can do for them. You can use a larger illustration to show more clearly what the product is and how it works. You can use more text material to tell why it is worth the purchase price. You can use larger type to make the copy easier to read and give the headline more impact. A more forceful overall impression can be made by increasing size alone.

Of a group of advertisements almost identical except for size, the larger ones will almost always do as well or better than the smaller versions. Also, the cost per reader for inquiries or sales generally will be the same, or lower, for large advertisements, despite the higher total cost of the space.

Large space, however, will not work wonders if the content of the advertisement is poor. Technique might also be a factor causing a smaller advertisement to outpull a larger one. "Technique," in this instance, may refer to such factors as stronger headlines, more clever themes, or more striking, attention-getting illustrations.

Evidence of the efficiency of smaller advertisements is provided in detail by the *Reader's Digest,* which naturally has an interest in convincing advertisers that their smaller advertisements can compete with bigger versions in magazines of conventional size. Although the *Digest* research is impressive, there are still, in most advertisers' minds, distinct advantages in working in larger units.

5. Don't obscure the benefit. The cute, the catchy, or the tricky may not work.

Being cute, catchy, or tricky is subordinate to conveying consumer benefits. Example: A transit card showing a squirrel saying *Take chances? Not me. I'm saving today* lost out to a more direct, more product-oriented card picturing a man saying *My bank—to 1,700,000 Canadians.*

Then, too, there was the lack of success of a comic strip treatment used by a maker of medical supplies such as adhesives, bandages, and back plasters. In tests against three different conventional advertisements, one of which was all type, the comic strip approach was a distinct loser. Comic strip illustrations for advertisements about shaving and house painting also showed up badly. The lesson is that a technique associated predominantly with entertainment is often not suitable for selling certain types of products. An advertiser who is considering the use of such a technique may find it desirable to run some tests to see how appropriate it is for the product.

This does not mean that the catchy picture or phrase should summarily be rejected—on the contrary, reader-stopping headlines and tricky illustrations have been outstandingly successful. Without such advertising there would be a gray sameness to advertising as a whole. That's the reason there's room for the "different" approach used by the Franklin Institute. When they changed formats from a conventional approach to an off-beat one, the difference in results was striking. In the conventional display advertisement, the headline said *Work for Uncle Sam.* This was far outshone by an advertisement that imitated a classified ad in which the small type was encircled. *Get on Uncle Sam's payroll* was given a bold, black line pointing to a coupon offering further information. This was an appropriate, simple way to sell a training course.

6. Get personal about the benefit, but don't get personal without a purpose.

It is generally accepted that formal, impersonal, and passive phraseology is undesirable for mass advertising. You are reminded constantly by copy experts to be—in most advertising—personal and informal. Still, being personal isn't always the key to interest and readership. For instance, an Eastman Kodak headline *Because photography is accurate to the last detail* was less personal but more successful than the one beginning *See what you can do with. . . .*

Once again, the advertiser should consider the individual circumstances, because the "be personal" advice can't always be applied. A writer of advertising to doctors or engineers will sensibly avoid too much familiarity in addressing such readers but will use ''you'' and ''your'' freely in writing trade advertising addressed to retailers.

Much depends upon whether the conversational feeling is appropriate for the advertising you're writing. If it is, then informality is desirable—certainly the case for most consumer print advertisements and all radio advertising.

Using ''your'' or ''you'' prominently doesn't necessarily guarantee anything. For example, seventeen advertisements doing so were tested against seventeen others that did not. Eight of the ''you'' advertisements were successful, but nine of the other ads were, too. No earth-shaking conclusions may be drawn here, but the figures back the point that the mere inclusion of personal words is no certain route to success.

If an advertisement can plainly and specifically show that the product is of interest to the reader, there is no absolute necessity to shout ''hey you'' to attract attention. Nevertheless, in most consumer advertising, personal and informal writing is desirable. In much of business advertising, on the other hand, this is not true.

What To Do To Get Attention, Create Desire, and Get Action When You Write Advertisements

Attention and interest factors are closely related in advertising. First, you attract the attention of possible readers; then, you invite them to read the message by switching quickly from mere eye catching to interest building. Most frequently, attention and interest are developed through headline and illustration treatment. After that, the first paragraph of copy is simply a transition from the ideas conveyed by the headline and illustration.

ATTENTION

In order to tell anyone about something, you first must get attention. This is true in personal conversation, mass communication, and advertising. Attention is meaningless, however, if it is not directed toward the product you're selling. Thus, it makes sense to properly draw the attention of the flip-and-run reader or the dial-turning television viewer to your message.

Advertisements that draw reader attention directly to a product benefit capture that interest more solidly than those that use attention-getting techniques merely for the sake of getting interest per se. Accordingly, a headline is more likely to attract attention if it promises a shortcut to a housewife scanning the shopping news. In a business publication, an illustration that visibly portrays a manufacturing cost cutter will be more likely to attract the attention of management-minded readers.

Importance of Attention Getting Varies with Audiences

Although attention getting has an effect on advertising results in all media, it is more important in some media than in others, especially in situations where you have a captive audience.

Consider a highly rated television show that holds you captive up to the moment the commercial flashes on the screen. Your attention is assured, but it may vanish quickly if the message doesn't offer an immediate promise of reward. Attention getting is more important to the television advertiser who uses a station break following the final commercial of a preceding program. Such an advertiser cannot rely on the same degree of captivity as the one above.

Magazine and newspaper advertisers have a greater problem in capturing reader attention. Because there is nothing of the captive audience here, such advertisers fight for attention, especially when they face competing advertisements on the same or adjoining pages.

Physical Elements Play a Part

Size, color, and unusual treatments attract attention, but a mere increase in size, the addition of color, or a switch to more unusual illustrations may not be enough. These techniques are successful in attracting attention only if they make the promise of a benefit more apparent to the audience. For example, we know from research that a dominant element such as a big illustration will increase attention. Still, to make this increased attention meaningful, the illustration should be relevant to the product and/or interests of readers.

Inevitably, we return to the principle that the intangibles of communication are more vital to successful rapport with readers, viewers, and listeners than are the physical means of expression. It is what you say and show that provides the key to attention—the ideas, the suggestions of value, the promise of value to be received. The secret lies in the idea values projected in the headlines and illustrations.

INTEREST

Attracting interest in your advertising depends on both the tangible aspects, such as physical attributes, and the intangible ones, such as appealing ideas.

The advertisements whose physical attributes do the best job of translating attention into interest are the ones that are mechanically the easiest to read. Such advertisements are organized so logically that information is easy for the reader to grasp. Picture-caption advertisements illustrate the point, as do those set in easy-to-read typefaces and those from which all distracting elements have been cut.

Still, the value of a physically perfect advertisement will be small if the ideas are mundane. It is the ideas conveyed by the first elements of an advertisement that either build or preclude sufficient interest for the reader to want to dig deeper into the message.

You will find some advertisements that clearly demonstrate to the reader the benefit of finding out what's good about the products and how they will fit his or her needs. These advertisements are high in general interest, promise a story, suggest an answer to a universal problem, touch the reader's self-interest, look as if they contain specific information of great interest, and contain believable illustrations of the product in action.

DESIRE

More than anything else, the purpose of an advertisement is to create a desire to own the product or use the service being advertised. As you will see from the researched advertisements in this book, most of the highly rated ones start immediately to build desire in headlines, illustrations, and introductory copy. Once again the importance of headline and illustration becomes apparent. One respected advertising agency head, in fact, told his creative people, "Put *everything* in the headline." To him, the reason for placing copy under a headline is to make the headline more important rather than draw attention to, or get results from, the copy itself. Few will agree that copy is *that* unimportant, arguing that it reinforces the ideas offered in the headlines and illustration. Copy, they say, reassures readers in many, and often new, ways that the

product will benefit them, sometimes to the point of convincing them that they can't do without it.

Results accrue from a composite of the effects created by headlines, illustrations, and copy. Yet the key almost always lies in the first impression conveyed in headlines and illustrations. If you can determine which advertisement the readers feel offers the greatest benefit, you will have found the one that achieves the most results.

Specific, relevant, unique, believable, and wanted benefits are the touchstones of desire creation in successful advertising.

ACTION

Although immediate action is often not expected from an advertisement, ultimate action (except for institutional advertisements) is always anticipated or hoped for. Because action is especially sought in mail order, or direct response, advertising, let us consider action in these terms.

In addition to direct sales, one measurement of effectiveness is the number of inquiries received. Inquiries come from people who presumably are good prospects. One way to spur inquiries is to use a coupon. Although couponed advertisements will generally outpull couponless ones, this is not always true—a couponless advertisement may have offered a benefit more relevant to the kind of people who were logical prospects for what was offered in the coupon.

You will also find instances in which smaller advertisements produced more inquiries than larger ones, and some cases in which larger advertisements were better at spurring action. A seeming contradiction? Not if you recognize that the mechanics of space size are not so important as the mental impact delivered by the idea quality of the content.

Moral: If you can use a larger space to create a picture of greater benefits, use it; but if you can't, use smaller advertisements more frequently. As the Newspaper Advertising Bureau has pointed out over and over again in its studies of copy effectiveness in newspapers, it's content that counts.

Another action question relating to mail order: Will inquiry returns drop if you charge for the sample or booklet offered? This question comes up when an advertiser offers something of value in general media. Such an advertiser usually wants to limit inquiries to logical prospects. Putting a nominal price on the offer is one way to make sure that inquiries will come from prospects only. Still, an advertiser hesitates to impose any block (even a small price) in the way of customer action.

In general, the results seem to vary more with what is offered than with the price of action. A charge for a worthwhile offer does not seem to reduce inquiries. Furthermore, in many cases of free offers, advertisers stress that there is no charge but neglect to put proper emphasis on the offer itself. It sometimes seems advisable to stress the value of the offer and play down the price or the fact that the offer is free.

All advertising is designed to produce sales in the long run, and only a small portion is aimed at direct orders obtained through advertising. As a rule, the copy researcher does not have actual sale results with which to demonstrate the effectiveness of advertisements. In mail order, the researcher has a solid measure of success—the number of orders obtained. This puts mail order in a class apart from other advertising.

When asking people to buy through mail order, you must give them the whole story. Unlike general advertising, where samples or displays of the merchandise in stores can complete the sale, nothing can be left to the imagination. Usually, therefore, the urge to action must be stronger in mail order advertising that solicits direct orders than in advertising that offers information or a free sample. In the former, the customer is more reluctant, because his or her action requires parting with cash.

Advertisements that pass the sales test include some features that might not be necessary or advisable in advertisements that are designed only to bend consumer attitudes more favorably toward a future purchase. Mail order advertisements are judged on the basis of their primary function: to obtain immediate sales. Some of the lessons learned from mail order advertisements can be applied—at least in part—to all advertising.

Some mail order advertisers first develop inquiries and then make a sale through a prepared follow-up. When that is the case, the mail order advertiser maintains records that relate inquiries to sales, thus making it possible to trace sales back to the advertisements that produced them, however indirectly. This gives the advertiser an opportunity to qualify inquiries and to find out not only what kind of copy will produce the *most* inquiries, but also what kind of copy will produce the *best* inquiries. The two do not always match.

Book advertisers are consistent testers. They have found that it pays to test every new book, and with new books being offered all the time, they have been strong users of big newspaper split runs, with which they compare individual parts of their advertisements such as headlines, illustrations, or general layouts. They can also use splits to determine what kind of people are the most logical customers for the books, thus allowing them to aim at the most productive market.

SUMMARY

The most important element in producing sales results is the benefit to the customer described in advertising. It is the strong benefit that leads to more attention, interest, desire, and, ultimately, action. Gimmicks, gadgets, and technique are distinctly subordinate to strong benefits.

Note that the mail order advertiser who piles benefit upon benefit, makes the value to the consumer most evident, unique, and believable, and makes such value and benefit the most easily obtainable is the one who wins out.

PACT Principles of Copy Testing

In 1982, twenty-one of the major U.S. advertising agencies issued a public statement called PACT (Positioning Advertising Copy Testing). PACT represented their consensus on the fundamental principles underlying a good copy testing system. These principles provide a foundation for understanding the use of advertising research.

The following advertising agencies[1] sponsored PACT: N. W. Ayer, Inc.; Ted Bates Worldwide, Inc.; Batten, Barton, Durstine & Osborne, Inc.; Benton & Bowles, Inc.; Campbell-Mithun, Inc.; Dancer Fitzgerald Sample, Inc.; D'Arcy-MacManus & Masius, Inc.; Doyle Dane Bernbach, Inc.; Grey Advertising, Inc.; Kenyon & Eckhardt, Inc.; KM&G International, Inc.; Marschalk Campbell-Ewald Worldwide; Marsteller, Inc.; McCaffrey and McCall, Inc.; McCann-Erickson, Inc.; Needham, Harper & Steers, Inc.; Ogilvy & Mather, Inc.; SSC&B: Lintas Worldwide; J. Walter Thompson Company; Young & Rubicam.

Principle 1:
A good copy testing system provides measurements which are relevant to the objectives of the advertising.

Advertising is used (as are all marketing tools) to contribute to the achievement of marketing objectives—whether they be for a product, a service, or a corporation. The industry recognizes (as exemplified by the landmark "DAGMAR"[2] study of the ANA) that the goal of advertising is to achieve specified objectives. It is further recognized that different advertisements can have a number of objectives, such as the following:

- Reinforcing current perceptions
- Encouraging trial of a product or service
- Encouraging new uses of a product or service
- Providing greater saliency for a brand or company name
- Changing perceptions and imagery
- Announcing new features and benefits

To be useful, a copy test for a given advertisement should be designed to provide an assessment of the advertisement's potential for achieving its stated objectives. Indeed, advertising objectives should be the first issue for discussion when a copy testing program is to be developed or a particular method is to be selected. In recognition of the fundamental importance of these objectives, every copy testing proposal and every report on results should begin with a clear statement of the advertising objectives.

Principle 2:
A good copy testing system is one which requires agreement about how the results will be used in *advance* of each specific test.

A primary purpose of copy testing is to *help* in deciding whether or not to run the advertising in the marketplace. A useful approach is to specify what are called "action standards" before the results are in. The following are some examples of possible action standards.

- Significantly improve perceptions of the brand as measured by _____.
- Achieve an attention level of no longer than _____ percent as measured by _____.
- Perform at least as well as (specify execution) as measured by _____.
- Produce negative responses of no higher than _____ percent as measured by _____.

The practice of specifying how the results will be used before they are in ensures that there is mutual understanding on the goals of the test and minimizes conflicting interpretations of the test once the results are in.

Moreover, prior discussion allows for the proper positioning of the action standards, since the copy test results are not, in most cases, the sole information used in deciding whether to use a particular advertisement. The results of any given copy test should be viewed in the context of a body of learning. Thus, prior discussion should take into account the following:

- How well the particular copy testing method used relates to the objectives of the advertising

- The *range* of results which are realistically achievable for the advertising approach used and for the brand or company in question

- The entire search context (including other types of studies) for the tested ad and for similar ads

A discussion of these issues prior to initiating a copy test provides benefits for both the advertiser and the agency. It minimizes the risks inherent in using copy test results in a mechanistic way, isolated from other learning. It maximizes the opportunity to draw upon the learning and seasoned judgment of the advertiser and the agency as both parties reach for the best possible advertising.

Principle 3:
A good copy testing system provides *multiple* measurements, because single measurements are generally inadequate to assess the performance of an advertisement.

With the exception of corporate advocacy advertising, it is commonly believed that the ultimate measurement by which advertising should be judged is its *contribution* to sales. But the complexity of the marketing process and the constraints of time and money usually preclude rigorous testing—that is, testing which can separate the effects of advertising from the many other factors that influence sales and thereby provide an estimate of the sales contribution of a given advertisement prior to a national launch. Nor is there any universally accepted single measurement which can serve as a surrogate for sales.

Moreover, the communication process is complex. To understand this process, and to learn from each successive test, it is necessary to use multiple measures—measures which reflect the multifaceted nature of communications. However, the inclusion of multiple measures should not imply that all measures have equal weight in evaluating the advertising. As noted previously, in advance of each test, agreement should be reached as to the relative importance of the various measurements in judging the acceptability of the tested execution.

Principle 4:
A good copy testing system is based on a model of human response to communications—the *reception* of a stimulus, the *comprehension* of the stimulus, and the *response* to the stimulus.

PACT agencies view advertising as performing on several levels. To succeed, an advertisement must have an effect:

- On the "eye," on the "ear": *It must be received* (RECEPTION)

- On the "mind": *It must be understood* (COMPREHENSION)

- On the "heart": *It must make an impression* (RESPONSE)

It therefore follows that a good copy testing system should answer a number of questions. Listed below are examples of the kinds of questions relevant to these communications issues. The order of the listing does not relate to priority of importance. As discussed in the preceding principles, priorities will vary depending on the objectives of the specific advertising being tested.

Reception
  —Did the advertising "get through"?
  —Did it catch the consumer's attention?
  —Was it remembered?
  —Did it catch his or her eye? His or her ear?

Comprehension
  —Was the advertising understood?
  —Did the consumer "get" the message?
  —Was the message identified with the brand?
  —Was anything confusing or unclear?

Response
  —Did the consumer accept the proposition?
  —Did the advertising affect attitudes toward the brand?
  —Did the consumer think or "feel" differently about the brand after exposure?

—Did the advertising affect perceptions of the brand?

—Did the advertising alter perceptions of the set of competing brands?

—Did the consumer respond to direct action appeals?

Another area of response measurements relates to executional elements. PACT agencies agree that it is useful to obtain responses to these elements of an advertisement.

Executional Diagnostics: Questioning about consumers' reactions to the advertising execution (e.g., perceived differentiation from other advertising, reactions to music, to key phrases, to presenters or characters, to story elements, etc.) can provide insight about the strengths and weaknesses of the advertising and why it performed as it did.

PACT agencies use different measures to address the issues in these four areas. However, they are all based on the same fundamental understanding of the communication process.

Principle 5:
A good copy testing system allows for consideration of whether the advertising stimulus should be exposed more than once.

Extensive experimentation in the field of communications and learning has demonstrated that learning of test material is far higher after two exposures than after one—and that subsequent exposures do not yield as large an increase as that between the first and second exposure.

In light of the experimental work, PACT agencies share the view that the issue of single versus multiple exposures should be carefully considered in each test situation. There are situations in which a single exposure would be sufficient—given the objectives of the advertising and the nature of the test methodology. There are other situations where a single exposure could be inadequate—particularly high risk situations, subtle or complex communications, or questioning about executional diagnostics.

Principle 6:
A good copy testing system recognizes that the more finished a piece of copy is the more soundly it can be evaluated and requires, as a minimum, that alternative executions be tested in the same degree of finish.

Experience has shown that test results can often vary depending on the degree of finish of the test executions. Thus, careful judgment should be used in considering the importance of what may be lost in a less than finished version. Sometimes this loss may be consequential; sometimes it may be critical.

The judgment of the advertising creators should be given great weight as to the degree of finish required to represent the finished advertisement for test purposes. If there is reason to believe that alternative executions would be unequally penalized in preproduction form, then it is generally advisable to test them in a more finished form. If alternative executions are tested in different stages of finish within the same test, then it is impossible to ensure that the results are not biased due to the varying degrees of finish.

Principle 7:
A good copy testing system provides controls to avoid the biasing effects of exposure context.

Extensive work in the field of communications and learning has demonstrated that the perception of and response to a stimulus is affected by the context in which the stimulus is presented and received.

In the case of advertising, it has been demonstrated, for example, that recall of the same commercial can vary depending on a number of conditions—such as, whether exposure to the commercial:

- Is off-air versus on-air
- Is in a cluttered reel of commercials versus a program context
- Is in one specific program context versus another specific program context

Thus, PACT agencies share the view that it is imperative to control the biasing effects of variable exposure contexts.

Principle 8:
A good copy testing system is one that takes into account basic considerations of sample definition.

- The testing should be conducted among a sample of the target audience for the advertised product. Limiting testing to the general population without provision for separate analysis of the target audience can be misleading.

- The sample should be representative of the target audience. To the degree that the sample drawn does not represent the target audience, the users of the research should be informed about the possible effects of the lack of representativeness on the interpretation of test results.

- The sample should take into account any geographical differences if they are critical to the assessment of the performance of a brand or service.

- The sample should be of sufficient size to allow a decision based on the obtained data to be made with confidence.

Principle 9:
A good copy testing system is one that can demonstrate reliability and validity.

To provide results which can be used with confidence, a copy testing system should be:

- *Reliable.* It should yield the same results each time that the advertising is tested. If, for example, a test of multiple executions does not yield the same rank order of performance on test/retest, the test is not reliable and should not be used to judge the performance of commercials. Tests in which external variables are not held constant will probably yield unreliable results.

- *Valid.* It should provide results which are relevant to marketplace performance. PACT agencies recognize that demonstration of validity is a major and costly undertaking requiring industrywide participation. While some evidence of predictive validity is available, many systems are in use for which no evidence of validity is provided. We encourage the cooperation of advertisers and agencies in pursuit of this critical need.

Interviews with Experts: Answers to Common and Important Questions about Advertising

This section presents interviews with some leading advertising authorities. They discuss candidly and informally various aspects of advertising, with special emphasis on creative matters.

Also included is an interview with the late George Gallup, which appeared in the previous editions of *Which Ad Pulled Best?* It is repeated largely as it was originally given, although some dated material has been deleted. Because it provides valuable insights by one of the great authorities in communication, it has been included again. Furthermore, the principles expressed by Dr. Gallup are timeless in their application.

In some instances the questions asked of the experts are similar. It is interesting and valuable to see how different respondents answer the same questions and—in so many instances—to see how closely they agree on the basic principles of advertising and advertising creativity.

GEORGE GALLUP
GALLUP & ROBINSON, INC.

Q: *In the course of the years, have you found much change in the way advertising works—in the kind of advertising that works best?*

A: No, I wouldn't say so. The copywriters change. But the kind of copy that has always worked still works. The problem is not so much one of finding out what new appeals work better today as it is of educating the new people who are coming along all the time in the basic principles of advertising. And, as a matter of fact, the old-timers seem to need reminding every now and then of the basics. We have to keep reproving old truths in terms of new products and new markets.

Q: *In the course of your experience with advertisers— and particularly with their advertising agencies—has any particular weak spot in the whole process of presenting sales ideas in advertising struck you as most needing correction?*

A: Well, I suppose there are a lot of weak spots. I'd say that the most greatly overlooked opportunity is that of advertising products. We find an awful lot of advertisers seem to be afraid to tell people about their products. But the public is very interested in products. They want to know all about these products that they can buy.

We have too much advertising that starts out talking about something else that is presumably of great general interest to prospective customers and then, after an involved transition, gets around to admitting that something's for sale. Actually, people read ads because they want to know what's for sale.

Q: *You say that people want to know about prices and about what's new in products and about what products will do. Would you say that any one of these elements is most important?*

A: No, because it depends on the product, on competition in the field, and on the different interest levels of different kinds of merchandise—and on a lot of other things. But I would say that there's an awful lot more news about products than many advertisers recognize. The opportunity is there for copy people to search out newsy things about products. A new price is in itself news. A new product is news. A new ingredient is news. A way of making a product stronger is news. There are a million and one things about products that relate to the benefits to be secured from buying them that are news. It's up to the copy people to wring this information out of the production people who know the facts but who don't realize their [the facts] value to advertising.

Q: *Is it the words, then, that are used in advertising copy that make the difference? Does the phraseology?*

A: No, not words or phrases, but *ideas*. That's what distinguishes, perhaps more than anything else, the advertising that penetrates from that which does not get under the skin of the people who see or read or hear it. The important thing is to present ideas forcefully. Words and images are the vehicles, of course, for all expression. But they are no good unless they mean something worthwhile to the folks on the receiving end.

Q: *Could you be a little more specific in what you mean by the forceful presentation of ideas?*

A: This big difference between advertisements—it's not one of using magic words. Boast copy is no good, no matter how many so-called magic words are strewn all the way through it. Proof copy, on the other hand—that is, believable proof copy—is the kind of thing that sticks with people. Demonstrations always have been effective. The before-and-afters are magic, not because of the words used or the size of the pictures so much as because of the magic in the idea, the proof of value.

One of the most interesting things about this whole question is that the kind of advertising that is most effective is the kind that is approved by the general public. The advertisements that cause complaints by the public are those that miss the boat—the boastful advertisements, the ones with the lack of proof, the ones that are cluttered up with ''adiness'' rather than performing the service for which advertising is ideally suited: telling people about the true benefits of merchandise.

Q: *How about the physical appearance of advertisements? Is there any general criterion that separates the good from the bad advertising in this respect?*

A: I guess the most generally applicable rule of thumb would be to separate advertisements into those with gimmicks and those without. The gimmicky advertisements usually don't work. Gimmicks tend to get in the way of idea expression.

By this I mean all kinds of gimmicks: trick headlines, color just for the sake of adding something extra, unusual typography, excessive use of tint block, copy patches that mutilate a main illustration, crazy pictures that have no relation to the product being sold. These things create ''adiness''; they take away from the clear expression of the many things about products that are of very great interest to the public.

Q: *Along these lines, it seems as though quite a lot of advertisers believe that they have to entertain as they sell. Aren't many of these gimmicks put in for entertainment value of a sort?*

A: I suppose many of the gimmicks are put in for entertainment value. But the thing is that people don't read advertisements to be entertained so much as to learn something about the products. It all comes back to the lack of appreciation of the interest of the public in merchandise—not just plain old merchandise, but new merchandise, new things about merchandise, new ways to use merchandise. There's plenty of entertainment value of a sort in the products, provided the copy writer is smart enough to find it and present it in a forthright and interesting manner.

Q: *Do you find that in a medium such as TV (technologically so far removed from, say, magazine advertising) the kind of copy approach that is most effective is very different from those that you have found resultful in other media?*

A: No, not really. In television there is the difference that results from having a captive audience to start with. You can jump right into the selling copy without having to snag attention first. The attention is there, so you go directly into the interest and desire-building process. Tricky wind-ups and abstruse lead-ins are usually a waste of valuable time in TV commercials. Additionally, in television you have the added dimensions of sound and motion to help. But aside from these considerations, the basics of persuasion are the same.

Q: *How long has Gallup & Robinson been testing TV commercials?*

A: We have been operating a television service—serving regular clients in this respect—since November of 1951. For about two years before that time, we were developing the research methods we use.

Q: *Could you describe in very general terms what those methods are?*

A: Very briefly, our methods of judging TV impact are of the same nature as those we apply in studying the impact of magazine advertisements. We concern ourselves with the thoughts and feelings a person has when an advertiser tries to register his sales message with him or her. We are looking at how well the advertising succeeds in making an impression and doing it in a persuasive fashion.

Q: *Do you find much difference in the impact made by different TV commercials?*

A: Oh, yes—a tremendous amount of difference. On average we experience a more than six-to-one difference in the levels of recall and persuasion. And then, of course, we get wide range in the playback of the selling messages and in the conviction, believability, and involvement that become apparent. You've got to keep in mind that the advertiser is paying the same amount of money to reach each of these levels of effectiveness.

Q: *How did the G&R Impact methodology evolve?*

A: At Young & Rubicam, we gained important insights about the methodology itself. While readership findings proved to be extremely helpful in reaching a larger audience with the advertiser's message, they did not provide all the information that was needed to produce effective advertising. The findings did not, for example, reveal how many of those who had seen or read given advertisements registered on the copy message or, for that matter, on the brand name. Nor did they shed light on the buying urge created by the copy.

To bridge this gap, a series of experiments was undertaken during the late 1930s and the early 1940s. This experimentation resulted in the development of the Impact method, which sought to move beyond reading and noting data and to measure such factors as registration of brand name and such qualitative parameters as idea communication and urge to buy. The new method could be used not only with print but with broadcast advertising as well. The first test of the method was a stripped-down copy of the April 16, 1945, issue of *Life* magazine with test ads "tipped-in." While we were working on these experiments at Young & Rubicam between 1945 and 1947, Dr. Claude Robinson, who founded Opinion Research Corporation (ORC), was conducting similar studies with a magazine called *Space*.

This experimentation eventually lead to the Impact method, which was fully in place by 1945. In 1947 I left Y&R to join Claude Robinson in a new venture called Gallup & Robinson to carry on research in advertising.

Q: *As you look back over your career in research, would you give us your impressions of the various trends or changes that have occurred?*

A: There have been many, many schools, one succeeding the other, in the history of copy research, when everybody ran this way and then ran that way. Of course, this is true in every field; one school succeeds another. But I think there's a trend back to the basics—not only in the United States, but all around the world. The first job of advertising is to get seen and read and then to change people's attitudes toward it.

Q: *How would that translate itself in terms of either research techniques or research philosophies?*

A: I don't think it would change the philosophies. The techniques need to be refined and improved. This whole problem of isolating and weighing the influence of advertising on a sale is a very sticky problem and always has been. You're trying to isolate advertising and its influence; you're trying to sort it out from a hundred other identifiable factors. I think it can be done, and it's amazing to me that more people aren't studying from year to year the advertising that is succeeding and what the factors are that are common to it as opposed to the advertising which demonstrably isn't succeeding.

Q: *How should an advertiser evaluate how effective his or her advertising is?*

A: Almost every campaign, to begin with, has specific objectives. The whole process of advertising is designing a strategy that will create a sale. You can find out if the strategy is working. Are you changing people's minds about this particular fact about the product? You can measure that. Every advertiser, even if he spends only a few thousand dollars, should demand some kind of evidence of the effectiveness of his advertising. And I am shocked, really, that sometimes advertisers spend millions of dollars without demanding that kind of evidence.

Q: *Of course, there are various schools of copy testing.*

A: And every school claims to be "the" school. But I think that the most useful, truthful way of thinking of copy testing is to regard all of the methods as useful and serving a given purpose. There isn't any method that will cover the waterfront. This is the mistake all schools of thought make. They believe if they find a cure for headache it will also cure flat feet; but one must know the limitations of each method. Being a good copy researcher is a matter of knowing exactly what each method will do, what its strengths are, and what its limitations are and not trying to come to some overall conclusion that if it's good in this area it has to be great.

Q: *What would you say is the major issue in survey research?*

A: Sampling obviously has to be number one. In the first part of this century, it was bad sampling that made the *Literary Digest* come up with the most inaccurate poll results in history, an error of 19 percentage points on a presidential election. They were sampling by mail and sampling people who had telephones and automobiles, which at that time was relatively atypical. We changed that to quota sampling up to 1948. Then our mistake, our election of Tom Dewey instead of Truman in 1948, was due largely to timing factors. At that point in history, we had to stop about ten days to two weeks before the election. After 1948 we had to invent ways of polling up through Saturday noon before election, because there are significant changes in those last few days. Now we can be accurate to tenths of percentage points.

TED BELL
YOUNG & RUBICAM

Q: *Let's start with establishing a definition of advertising—what you think it is, and what does it do?*

A: Some people have called it the engine of capitalism. Advertising creates awareness of products and business services. Without advertising, nobody would know that there were six kinds of cars to buy, or toothpaste or soap. So advertising is the spreading of information; it's communicating news about products and also creating emotions about products in the marketplace.

Q: *What role does advertising play in the buying process?*

A: It creates demand and disseminates information.

Q: *Let's turn the question around a little bit. Why do people look at advertising?*

A: Well, first, advertising is ubiquitous. It's everything—television, print, newspapers. You can't shut it out. But the reason it is so present is that people crave information. They want to know about what they can buy. They are inquisitive. It's a part of human nature to want to know what's out there.

Q: *Are there differences between print advertising and television advertising, or are they really the same things just in different forms?*

A: I think they're closely related. A good ad, regardless of the media, presents an idea in a fresh way so that somebody will do something or think about a product or service in a different way. And for me, the best advertising ideas have a directness and simplicity to them. That's why print is such a good medium to work in. With print you have only the idea, a pen or pencil, and piece of paper. Too often what happens in broadcast and television is production and music and surface imagery take the place of an idea. You can't get away

with that in print. The best advertising ideas have to be able to be done in print, or they may not be good ideas.

Q: *Are there certain types of ideas that are easier or better to convey in print versus TV?*

A: Yes and no. There are some things we wouldn't really want to do a commercial for. In the case of something that is highly technical, where there's a lot of technical writing or information that needs to be conveyed, we wouldn't want to be in a 30-second commercial. More likely, the idea can come alive in both media. There's a famous Volkswagen print ad from the old agency Doyle Dane Bernbach, where I started. It showed the lunar landing module descending to the moon with a headline text saying, "It's ugly, but it gets you there," together with the Volkswagen logo. Although the ad was not made into a TV commercial, you can imagine that it would make an equally great commercial. You would see the surface of the moon and, all of a sudden, this little thing comes down into the frame and starts to get lower, lower, lower—you hear the sound effects, and you see this funny-looking thing, and it sits and settles on the surface of the moon and the dust flies up, and a little super comes up and says, "It's ugly but it get you there." That is a great television commercial. The idea is the star, so it works in both media.

Q: *If you're a U.S. company, why do you do print advertising?*

A: Well, a lot of small companies do print because it's what they can afford. If you're a larger company and can afford both, I always recommend they do both. Let's say you're an automobile company. A 30-second commercial could be used to show beautiful running shots of a car so you see how beautiful the car is. A print ad could give you more information about the car to justify the $30,000 investment. You're not gonna just say "That's a pretty car. I'll go buy it." So that's one way print and TV work together.

Q: *How does the audience to which the ad is directed fit into the process of creating the advertising?*

A: You try to have this image of the market in your mind. Really good creative people have very good instincts about how most people think, how people will react to a given theme. It's hard to describe, but if I come up with an idea, I don't know how I know this, but I just know it will work. You have a feel for whether people will think it's funny, whether they'll understand it, and whether they'll like it. You have to have a sense of human nature and enormous common sense. I think the skills necessary for a creative person are intelligence, taste, and imagination. If you've got those, you'll be a pretty good advertising person.

Q: *When you're thinking about an ad, how does the process evolve?*

A: I start writing for myself as a member of my audience. If I don't think an idea's funny or fresh, I'm not gonna show it to anybody else. I put myself in the position of someone sitting at home by myself reading a magazine. Would I think the ad was funny, would I like it or believe it or hate it? Just write for your audience. If you're writing a financial ad that's going to run in *Fortune*, you're going to write a different ad than if you're trying to sell soap to a woman in Des Moines who's interested in getting her son's boxer shorts clean. One of the first things you get in an advertising strategy is the target. For example, say kids 18–24. Okay, now you've helped me to start to figure out how I'm gonna think about this. I'm probably not going to do something cerebral; I'll probably do something with energy and fun. You think about the target. It puts you right into it.

Q: *Can you take us through the process that you go through to develop a piece of print advertising?*

A: Usually it begins with the client. They brief you on the problem—whether it's the lack of awareness for the product, a lack of differentiation for it, or low esteem. Then you go back and say, "All right, how are we gonna fix this? What's the solution to this problem?" And, typically, you create a strategy. You target the audience, say, men ages 20 to 30, upper income, some college. Then you develop a strategy, say, to convince the target these glass apples are the best glass apples in the world. You dig into the product to see why it's better, and then you come up with a strategic proposition. You may not explicitly see this in the advertising, but it's the foundation upon which the advertising is built that says what people need to hear about this product in order to want it. There are support points for it—the glass apple—Old World craftsmen, pure lead, etc. Then you go back to the client and you say, "Here's the strategy. We think we should talk about the apple's pure lead crystal and Old World craftsmanship." It's important for people to agree to the strategy up front so you don't have to spin your wheels. The strategy is given to the creative people to come up with an interesting way to talk about pure lead crystal and Old World craftsmanship.

Q: *One often hears about rational advertising versus emotional advertising, or feature/benefit versus im-*

age. *How relevant are these type of distinctions? Are they important, and if they are, what do they mean in terms of the type of advertising that you try to create?*

A: They're all relevant, and they're all linked, and it depends on the product and category. You wouldn't want to be real rational about soft drink advertising. You know, you wouldn't want to explain to me why 7UP is a great product in rational terms. You could do that and it would be funny, but then it's emotional advertising. All advertising is emotional in some way because you have an emotional response to it no matter what. Even when you feel that advertising is very rational, you are having an emotional response. You can't not have an emotion, whether it's I hate it, I love it, or I'm bored. But the key is to figure out what you want to say to people and then say it in a way that makes them like you. If people like you they're much more willing to listen to what you're saying. And even if they don't quite believe it, they'll still pick you over the other guy because they like you. Think about McDonald's. They didn't get to be the largest hamburger chain by telling people what was in the hamburger. They got there because they made people love McDonald's, and all McDonald's advertising is designed to reinforce that. That's not to say that you don't need to promote, but, basically, their mission is to make people like McDonald's more than the other guy.

Q: *How do you judge whether a print ad is effective? Do you look at the whole or do you look at the pieces?*

A: The first thing I ask myself is, "Will I stop and look at this ad if I were reading the magazine?" If I'm reading the magazine and won't even look at it, then I don't even care what the ad says, because nobody's gonna pay attention to it. So the first question is, "Will it stop me?" Once I get past that point I say, "Is it compelling? Is it interesting? Is it funny? Does it tell me something I don't know? Does it have an idea, or is it just a headline and a picture? Is it artfully done? Is it intelligently written?" The great Bill Bernbach had a theory, and I think he was right. He believed advertising was part of the culture, and it's incumbent upon advertising agencies not to litter up the highways and byways of everybody's mind and physical space with junk. That underscores the place for intelligence and taste in advertising.

Q: *How do you know when a piece of advertising becomes stale or needs to change?*

A: You just seem to know, but there's a danger that you're so close to it that you and the client get tired of it before the public, which doesn't see it as much as you do.

Q: *Some people think that the advertising environment is becoming more cluttered and people are being bombarded by all sorts of different approaches. What implications does this have for the advertising messages that you create?*

A: There was a time in the not too distant past where the whole country sat down and watched the Ed Sullivan Show all the way through. To sell something you could go on the Ed Sullivan Show and count on everybody seeing your message. That doesn't even come close to happening anymore. It's totally fractured, and there's far more advertising than ever before. You've got to stand out. You gotta stand up and be counted and get somebody to know you. Too much of today's advertising is safe and conservative, and that contributes to many messages not getting noticed. It's why you have to "break through" first.

Q: *I've wondered if this more cluttered environment has implications for the relative importance of the individual executions versus the campaign itself. For large brands especially, like AT&T, you pay less attention to each individual ad, but together as a whole, all of the execution create a presence.*

A: Individual or cumulative. Both are important. People form their opinions not based on any one execution but on the totality of the messages you're sending to them. I've had clients tell me, "You don't understand. We don't do image advertising." I disagree. Every ad you do is an image ad, because every time you run any commercial people are going to have an image of you. So if you're doing clunky, boring advertising, you're a clunky, boring brand. You know, they're going to form an image of you based on what you tell them—what you send out there. You have a vision of Nike based on a lot of different sensory input that you had over the years from their advertising.

Q: *Is there any one myth of advertising that you'd like to dispel?*

A: Yes, that it's easy; it's really hard. It's easy to do sloppily. It's easy to do in an ordinary fashion. But it's hard to do something really good.

Q: *For someone who is starting out now and thinking of getting into the creative side of the advertising business, what skills would you like to see them have?*

A: You have to be a keen observer of human nature. You have to have a lot of common sense. You have to have a sense of humor and can't take yourself too seriously, and I think you've gotta have creative talent, which you can't go out and get at the store. Really good art directors are usually great copywriters, and terrific copywriters usually have a lot of taste and know what something should look like—what Leo Burnett called the "fitness of things." Although they're two discrete skills, when you are really talented in either one, you usually are pretty good in the other. Funny, isn't it?

ROY GRACE
GRACE & ROTHSCHILD

Q: *What does successful advertising do?*

A: There are several different levels on which you can answer this question. You could say advertising motivates the consumer to purchase your product. But that's an easy answer and an obvious one.

To truly answer the question, you have to get into that whole mysterious area of what comprises advertising and what motivates people. What's important here is that you have the reader or viewer participate in your advertising. We want people to get involved in the advertising, we want them to think, we want to do things that are provocative, that force them to wrap their minds around our proposition. All successful advertising does that. Unfortunately, the vast majority of advertising gathers no response whatsoever. People just don't see it, they don't hear it, because it doesn't recognize that essential issue which is: you must get somebody involved, you must make them think or feel.

Q: *Could you position the role of advertising in the broader business context of the buying decision?*

A: Advertising, in its simplest terms, provides information. It tells me that there's a sale going on, it tells me that your product has front-wheel drive and fuel injection. It provides information to the consumer. So it is a voice for the product, a voice for the manufacturer. It is their way of communicating and telling the public what ingredients they have in their product, what the benefits of their product are. What it really replaces is the salesman in the store, or the store window, to a certain degree. It imparts information to the consumer.

Where advertising gets again more complex is in the real world, where most products exist on a parity level with their competition. What's the difference between Drink "A" and Drink "B"? There is no difference, and what advertising can do is create a difference. Advertising helps sell a product that may be on a parity with its competition. If the manufacturer is astute at choosing a good agency, he has bought himself a very forceful ally in selling his merchandise.

Advertising also helps improve products. When I improve a product, I use advertising to get out there as fast as I can to tell the world that I now have a new ingredient that gets your clothes whiter than they should dare be. This also alerts the competition that they've got to make a better product.

Q: *How is television advertising different from print advertising, and how are they the same?*

A: Television is an easier form to work in from a creative point of view. For one thing, your mistakes are easier to cover because of the medium's pace. You have an enormous asset that you don't have in print, and that's sound and music. You have the element of time, which works very much in your favor, so you can build dramatically. If you have to compare a 30-second commercial today with a printed page, in television you have 30 seconds to tell your message, while in print you have maybe a second and a half with a vague possibility that somebody will read the copy.

Print is a more difficult and rigorous discipline, and a lot of people can't do both. It's really interesting—some people can do television and have no concept of print, and some people can do print and have no concept of television. It's not that unusual to find that the reasons have to do with the person as an individual and his/her ability to "control."

There are certain people who can control everything on their desk. They can control the elements, the typography, the photography, the retouching, and so on. They feel very much in command, because they are dealing primarily with inanimate objects. When you get in the area of television, you're dealing sometimes with 50 or 100 people, and you're dealing with directors, producers, cameramen, gaffers, grips, and it's a constantly moving target. It's a different kind of control.

Q: *Are there situations where a print advertisement can have more impact than a television commercial? Do certain products or selling appeals work better in print than in television, and why?*

A: There are certain products where there is really a lot of information to be told and where 30 seconds just doesn't afford the time to communicate a decent amount of information. Print is far better in these situations. There is also a reality to print that often corresponds better with a certain kind of problem than television. Also, I might choose print because in this business, when everybody zigs, you zag. You might get an awful amount of leverage out of being in print when nobody else is. You may be able to *own* a magazine because nobody else is there. You have to look at the whole spectrum of possibilities and not at whether these things are better in either medium as an absolute.

But television is the favored medium now. In fact, when people talk about advertising today, they rarely talk about print. It always amazes me. I grew up in print and I love print, but I talk about television. Television is very seductive—you have the music, the motion, and the beautiful cinematography. I can make you cry in 30 seconds, or I can make you laugh in 30 seconds. The emotions are much more reachable in television than they are in print. In print, though it's possible, it is more difficult.

Q: *Does advertising "work better" with certain types of people?*

A: I would think not, unless you get to the end of the spectrum, where people absolutely and rigidly hate advertising of all sorts. It also depends on the product. The man who might not be interested in the Chivas Regal ad might be interested in an ad about a Rolls Royce. My mother wouldn't be interested in an ad about an IBM computer, but she would be interested in an ad on SOS Soap Pads. If the product's right for them, there's no reason why advertising shouldn't be right for them.

Q: *One often hears about informational versus emotional advertising. What do these concepts mean in terms of the advertising you create?*

A: Let's take the example of the Range Rover ad, "We brake for fish." All that this message is trying to convey is that the Range Rover is extremely capable off-road. From an intellectual point of view, we could simply say just that: the Range Rover is extremely capable off-road. But to capture the thought in these unimaginative and prosaic terms is rather dull. However, when you put the vehicle in an unusual off-road situation—like water—and you twist the familiar expression of "We brake for animals," you are communicating the same information on an emotional level. Therefore, it's much more disarming and memorable.

Q: *Is the use of emotion, as you're describing it, to draw the person into the ad or to make the message that you're trying to communicate more persuasive?*

A: Both. It's to draw them into the ad, to make the message more persuasive, and it must be relevant to the product. It can't just be a funny joke that has no relevance to the product—it has to come out of the product's basic reason for being. I believe in trying to make people laugh at your advertising, make them smile, make them feel something. I believe in that very strongly. It goes back to why people read magazines—they don't read them for the ads.

Q: *Does the same description apply if we are talking about television commercials?*

A: Absolutely.

Q: *What is the role of the creative person in creating?*

A: At Grace & Rothchild, a writer and an art director usually sit together, and, together, they come up with the concept, the idea, the headline, the picture. This team approach was one of the innovations that Bill Bernbach brought into this business.

Today, the lines of responsibility are almost, but not totally, blurred. Everybody writes and everybody art directs. What you really have is a team of two people sitting down and coming up with the ad, the commercial, everything. Every ad you'll see here at this agency was done essentially by two people, a writer and an art director.

Q: *What is the hardest part about creating a print ad?*

A: It's the idea—it's always the idea. The idea is the impossible wall to scale, always, until you do it, and then it's so easy. It's always that elusive goal that constantly stares at you through a blank sheet of paper and says it's impossible until it's there. It's always that. I'm sure if you ask any writer or art director they will tell you the same thing. It's terrifying sometimes.

Q: *In terms of the creative challenge, is there a difference between consumer and business-to-business advertising?*

A: No, they're absolutely the same. It's a problem with a solution, and if you know the problem and know who you're talking to, the solution has to be there.

Q: *Do you have a favorite way to describe the major components of print advertising and what they can do and how they should work together?*

A: What's important is that the ad works as an entirety. Another way to think about it is to say that there must be a beginning to every ad. There has to be a point on every page where the art director and the writer want you to start. Whether that is the center of the page, the top right-hand corner, or the left-hand corner, there has to be an understanding, an agreement, and a logical reason where you want people to look first. There has to be a logical progression to every ad. There has to be the place my eye goes first, the place it goes second, third, and so on.

Q: *What is the role of celebrities in print advertising?*

A: I believe in the use of celebrities only when they are relevant to the product. If you're going to use a 7-foot basketball star because you have a lot of headroom in your car, that makes a lot of sense. If you're going to use him to sell peanut butter, that makes no sense at all.

For the most part, celebrity advertising is borrowed interest. You don't want the consumer walking away from your advertisement thinking about the celebrity and not thinking about the product. The *product* should be the celebrity. Only if a celebrity is relevant to a product does it make sense to use one. The same that holds true in print holds true in television.

Q: *What about the role of humor in print advertising?*

A: If it's relevant to the product, humor is a wonderful selling tool. It's a way for people to like you, and I think that if they like you there's a better chance they'll buy you. But even today, humor isn't without its critics. It's very hard to do, and it's also risky. Perhaps because it's so personal, you open yourself to a punchline that nobody appreciates.

That's not only embarrassing, but advertisers can lose customers and agencies can lose clients that way.

Q: *Let me ask you about the role of coupons in print advertising.*

A: They're there for a very good reason. If you can get an instant sale, an instant customer, an instant prospect from your advertising, why not? I think you'd be mad not to. I think they make a lot of sense for a lot of products. A coupon is a way to buy the product, a coupon is a way to get more information about the product. Now what would you rather do if you had a choice—just build brand loyalty or sell the product and build brand loyalty? I would prefer to sell the product.

Q: *From a creative perspective, how do you decide on the size of the ad to be run?*

A: Obviously, this is a time when management perspective may be more important, but from a creative perspective, biggest is the best. Why share a page with someone else? The sheer square inches that confront you screens out your competition. There may be more efficiencies in smaller units. You may have a motivating reason to be very small, such as you have the smallest umbrella ever made and you want to highlight that point. Maybe the media corresponds to the creative idea. So bigger is not always better. But as a generality, I would say it is.

Q: *When is it time to start a new campaign?*

A: Hopefully, never. You always hear that the client or agency grows tired of a campaign before the consumers even see it. That's true all too often.

When you set out to do a campaign, a lot of people say, "This should last at least three years." For me, when you sit down to do a campaign, it should ideally last forever. There should never be, unless there are underlying reasons, any plan for this campaign ever changing. It should be built and manipulated to last forever.

Q: *Can you provide an illustration of a campaign that has been relatively timeless and how it has been modified from year to year to take advantage of changes in product or changes to market?*

A: Again, I would choose Land Rover as a good example. Although the campaign has only been running for not quite 10 years, it's demonstrated an enormous amount of flexibility. For example, when we first began working with Land Rover, it was a single product: Range Rover. It has now evolved into a three-product company, with the Defender and the Discovery. Each product has a different audience. Therefore, each audience must get a relevant message from that product, yet at the same time all the advertising must remain within the context of the same campaign. We've had to deal with Range Rover's price increasing from $30,000 when first introduced to $60,000 today. We've had to deal with a handful of competitors in the beginning to over 35 today. What allows this campaign to adapt to all these changing needs and keep prevailing in the marketplace is a sound fundamental strategy to begin with. The campaign has stayed the same, but changed.

Q: *What do you see as the major problems with the state of print advertising today?*

A: Everything now is beautifully packaged and very safe. I would rather see more of the extremes. I think we've had more great print and we've had more terrible print. We're missing a lot of the fire some of the ads used to have. Everything moves in cycles, and sooner or later the cycle has to begin again.

Q: *What do the changes to television—the zapping, the audience fragmentation—portend for print?*

A: Zapping and the 15-second commercial are probably the best friends that print has ever had. Anything that makes television less attractive to watch is going to make advertisers consider print more attractive.

On top of this, the emergence of special-interest magazines has made print into a much more exciting medium. It is also very helpful to an advertiser, be-cause you are being provided the opportunity to talk with somebody with a sharpened interest when they go through the magazine.

Q: *What is your favorite myth about advertising that you would like to dispel?*

A: That we have this insidious power to manipulate people through all types of hidden techniques, such as subliminal frames, anamorphic pictures, hidden persuaders, and things like that. I am constantly amazed by the number of otherwise intelligent people who subscribe to that incredible point of view.

Q: *In the fifties, Rosser Reeves said that the most dangerous word of all in advertising is "originality." Do you agree or disagree?*

A: I disagree violently with that. Let me answer that in a roundabout way. Going back 15 years or so, the word "creative" was somewhat of a dirty word. You couldn't use the word "creative" without being followed by the word "boutique," like Doyle Dane Bernbach, that creative boutique. To me the word "originality" is synonymous with creative. And creativity is what this business is about. The only way you're going to get somebody to look at your ad, whether it be in print or television, is to give them the proposition in a fresh and original way.

Originality is everything. It's the way you draw people in. It's the information you give them. It's the product. And if the product is original, it sets the stage for everything else, because everything should come from the product. Originality is great at any one of these levels, but it's mandatory in advertising, especially when you have a product that is nearly the same as everybody else's. How can I get you to listen to the same information over and over again unless I tell it to you in a fresh and original way, especially realizing that you're not reading this magazine or watching television because of our advertising?

Q: *One often hears of the concepts of positioning and brand personality or character. Could you talk about both of those concepts as they apply to your work?*

A: There is really no separation between the two. A brand obviously must have a position, it must have its place, its niche in the marketplace in order to survive, in order to thrive. That's imperative. A brand must have a personality, it must have a feeling, it must evoke some kind of a human response from the intended purchaser. And every advertiser must build a long-term personality for its brand. That goal is mandatory.

The position of the brand and the personality are inseparable, because when you sit down to position the brand you have to think of what is the appropriate tone for your advertising. Will that communicate the feeling that you want people to have about the product?

Q: *What advice do you have for new people coming into the industry?*

A: New people should try to understand what advertising appeals and doesn't appeal to them—and why. They should keep a list of the advertising they like: jot it down, tear it out of the magazine; find out the agencies who did it; also pull out the advertising they don't like, and find out the agency that did that. As a practical matter, never work for the agency whose advertising you don't like or respect. Accept no rules, I would tell them, except the one rule: Anything goes.

J.J. JORDAN
J. WALTER THOMPSON USA

Q: *How do you define advertising?*

A: Advertising at its best is a compelling invitation. It's not a coercion, it's not an imperative statement—it's an invitation.

Q: *What role does advertising play in the buying process?*

A: Good advertising plays two roles. When somebody has a really good product, the benefits of which are clearly demonstrable, advertising presents the case in a way that people will notice and remember. Advertising also creates an image for the product. Parity products like soft drinks and athletic wear are classic cases where advertising helps create a face or a personality to differentiate the brands. When someone is uncertain, an extra emotional connection may swing the sale. There are brands that are doing just fine without advertising, and there are brands that are doing okay despite poor advertising, but there are a lot of brands that could be doing much better with better advertising.

Q: *How do you know if advertising has been successful?*

A: Well, sales are definitely a key criteria for successful advertising. But, ultimately, advertising is about building or contributing to successful brands. People can ascribe identities or characteristics to some products and they can't to others, and advertising has a lot to do with making that difference. Nike has a personality. I'm not sure that Adidas has a personality anymore. Apple has a personality. Some computer brands are struggling to create one. Advertising is effective if the brand is starting to take on a character that people seem to like. There's an added value to the brand that is above and beyond the intrinsic value of the product.

Q: *Can you share an anecdotal story with us that shows the power of advertising?*

A: We did a couple of commercials for Lipton, the grand old man of tea. They've always had a canned iced tea beverage, but they entered a partnership with Pepsi and came out with a high-quality bottled tea called Lipton Original. We did some advertising for it under the tagline "This ain't no sipping tea" to emphasize the chuggability and thirst-quenching aspects. The campaign played against the target's expectations of Lipton Tea and put Lipton in a new light. They ran two 30-second spots during the Super Bowl that were both in the top ten in terms of likability and recall. It wasn't too long before Lipton's Iced Tea franchise overtook Snapple's nationally. The spots and their placement in the Super Bowl helped propel Lipton from being Dandy Don Meredith's tea right into the mainstream of an emerging powerful beverage category.

Q: *Let's turn it around a little, why do people look at advertising?*

A: A zillion reasons. They look at it depending on who they are and what the medium is. If I'm a ski buff and I'm leafing through *Ski* magazine or *Powder* magazine, I'm looking at advertising as if I'm shopping. On television, cable creates more and more targeted shopping-like opportunities. I'm not a fisherman, but I'm mesmerized by the cadence of fishing shows. If you watch a Saturday morning fishing program you'll see that somebody's out there producing dozens of fishing lure spots or tackle box spots. Some of them are great. And you know that most people watching those spots bring a keen interest and buying enthusiasm.

If I'm reading a more general interest magazine or watching Seinfeld or something, I look at the advertising because it's entertaining and relevant. It's like a door-to-door salesman. If you like the guy when you open the door, if he presents his case in a way that's meaningful and he seems to understand you, you're going to listen to what he says and he's more likely to make the sale. If the guy's off-putting, then he's probably not going to sell you—even if he's got something pretty good. Some research says that people pay more attention to car advertisements *after* they've bought a car. They look at it with some sort of self-validating hindsight. Sometimes you look at advertising because its truly aesthetic. The Fruitopia spots mesmerize me. Visually pleasing print can be like a poster. And sometimes advertising provides drama. We did some spots for E.P.T. where we documented people finding out on camera whether they were going to have a baby or not. If you think about it, E.P.T. is a relatively inexpensive product that, when used properly, provides you with a piece of information that changes the course of your life. We had a little setup section where couples talked about their hopes and aspirations. Then they take the test, they see the results, they react. It's wonderful. It's almost journalistic—and very compelling viewing. For every different category, for every different medium, there's a different reason people watch, and it's going to become even more complex and more fragmented as times evolve.

Q: *If you're a company, why do you use print advertising?*

A: It doesn't pay for most ski companies to advertise on television. You've got a relatively narrow audience and you know you can reach them efficiently in a ski magazine. Right off the bat, there's that ability to target. Secondly, there are a lot of companies that feel that print provides a better opportunity for message depth because you can write long copy and explain. This is especially true for technical products. Thirdly, some products benefit from the environment of the magazine. If I were trying to sell to young people, I might try to get on Fox or MTV, but I'd also want to be in *Rolling Stone* or in *Wired*. Print gives the advertiser a great degree of control over the environment their ad is in.

Q: *Are certain messages conveyed more easily in print than in television, or are they really both the same thing?*

A: The beauty of print is it forces you to condense. The best print ads have the brevity and punch of a good editorial cartoon: the visual and the headline are mutually dependent, and the whole is greater than the sum of its parts. Print forces you to put your advertising idea in a nutshell and provides the opportunity to get more in-depth than is probably cost-efficient on TV. On the other hand, TV lets you do some demonstrations that you can never do in print. TV gives you the element of time, even if it's only 30 seconds. Something can play out. You can reveal. If you see a gatefold or a spread in a magazine, that's a print way to recreate what you do in TV. If you have to reach a lot of people and you really want to make an event happen, generally TV is considered better. But ideally, there's nothing advertised on TV that couldn't be advertised well in print.

Q: *If you have both print and TV as part of what you're doing, what should the two be doing together or differently?*

A: You have to have some brand synergies. You want to make sure that both media are speaking with the same voice. Avoid confusing signals. For example, we did a campaign for Lever 2000, ''Lever 2000 for all your 2000 parts.'' The TV was a rhythmic, whimsical presentation of body parts, using a kind of a charming Dr. Seuss cadence and very clean looking families. The print ended up working very synergistically with the TV by juxtaposing two body parts, which was the essence of the Lever 2000 idea. Print boiled it down to a singly postery image, like a father's arm wrestling with a baby's arm. So they are related but a little different.

Convention sometimes portrays TV as the broad stroke, and print takes care of more targeted, more specific messages—more like sniper fire. And indeed, both media should act optimally for themselves, but you shouldn't be talking like W.C. Fields in one media and like George Bush in another.

Q: *How does the audience to whom the advertising is directed effect how much you think about advertising that you write?*

A: Targeting can be a trap, because it can lead you into simplistic answers if you're not careful. ''We're targeting youth, so let's do some of that rock 'n roll stuff, because that's what they like.'' I've found that the ads that appeal to youth most tend to be *smart* ads that appeal to everybody.

In general, though, understanding your product's role in your customer's life is imperative. If you're smart, you're getting beyond just ''women 18–25'' or whatever, and you're actually learning about how your target really relates to your category. The more you learn, the more likely you'll gain an unexpected insight that leads to a unique opportunity for your product. You've got to go beyond merely identifying the target, to learning how to talk to them.

Q: *Sometimes you hear the distinction between rational and emotional advertising or feature/benefit arguments and image advertising. Are those distinctions still relevant? Do they have implications for the types of advertising that you create?*

A: We talk about the head and the heart a lot. There are only a few products that can exist exclusively in one of those domains. Even the most imagistic stuff should have something underlining functionality or rational foundation. People always point to Nike ads as being image-laden. But when you look closely at what those spots are, you see they're product demonstrations for the entire 30 or 60 seconds: people running, playing, using the product, being healthy, and exuding end benefits. The line "Just do it" is one of those insight lines. They thought about the target. They thought about the inner voice. They thought about the exhortation that comes from within, and they made it their themeline.

There is some advertising that can be very effective just using the rational sale. But, generally, that advertising does not succeed in creating a brand and developing a long-term franchise. Remember, for most products the *brand* is the most valuable part of the franchise. Likewise, if you just go soft and imagey, your brand won't survive, because it will be hollow, irrelevant, and ultimately disappointing. The biggest kiss of death in marketing is to lure people in and then disappoint them with what they buy. The best advertising, of necessity, has to compel rationally and emotionally.

Q: *Can you describe the process an agency goes through to create a print ad?*

A: Well, it probably varies by agency, but here's what we do. First, with a marketing insight, we identify who we're talking to and the unique selling point of the ad. Sometimes it can be quite specific, or sometimes it reinforces what is being said in television. We come up with a very crystallized articulation of what the advertiser wants to do and say, which we call the Big Idea Brief. We try to do it in one sentence. Then the creative team takes the brief and, over a period for three or four weeks, creates. The ads are presented internally to the group head, and then to me, during which time they are edited and tweaked. Then we go to the client and say, "Here are three choices. We recommend this one."

Q: *Are the creatives involved in preparing this brief?*

A: Yes, definitely. One of their key contributions is helping to boil the brief down—especially for print, but also for TV, because there's only so much you can say in 30 seconds. We also help make sure that it's a brief that's creatively executable and not redundant with something someone else is saying.

Q: *What's the distinction between writers and art directors in today's creative environment?*

A: Today is much different that it was. If you go back to the fifties, you were in the days of "Ivy League writers" and "fine artist" art directors. An art director in an agency then was somebody who could do a lifelike oil painting. That's not the case now. Today, the two are much closer. All our art directors are trained conceptually now and have gone to some program or school. That's a little less so with the writers, because some do come in from other areas like liberal arts writing or journalism. But essentially, they're much closer to being two sides of the same coin; they're advertising people. I've had people come here and switch. Both crafts can be practiced and honed, but somebody needs to be more involved with the visual issues and somebody needs to specialize in a fresh voice. Ultimately, it's the benefits from two people in a room working together—with give and take and the opportunity to bounce ideas "What if we did" or "How 'bout this"—that matters most. The personal chemistry probably has as much to do with it as anything else.

Q: *You mentioned the computer earlier. How is the computer changing how ads are created?*

A: Hopefully, we're now through what I called an infatuation period with the computer, where you saw a lot of strange solutions that existed simply because the computer could make them. Both in art direction and writing, you need to start conceptually and loose. We still see a lot of good-looking stuff that's fundamentally flawed because it's been rushed into finishing or type choice or the arty placement of icons before the *idea* was refined.

Q: *When someone brings you a print ad to look at, what do you look for? How do you judge whether it works or not? Do you look at only the whole? Do you look at pieces?*

A: Well, that depends. Sometimes one piece is glaringly great and the others glaringly wrong. Generally, what I look for in print is a whole that's greater than the sum of its parts. When a great headline is put with the visual, is the ad better than the headline by itself? I want an ad to make me smile or move me on some level. I want it to be compelling—a compelling invitation to consider the product or the service or offer. I was a fine arts major, so I tend to want visually distinctive or striking ads. A New Yorker cartoon is a good model. There are some that can exist without any line of copy at all because the visual is so funny. There are some where the line is so funny that the visual is just a couple talking. But in the best cartoons, the two pieces are entwined and are just wonderful together.

Q: *When you're looking to hire someone on the creative side, what do you expect people to have already learned before they come to you?*

A: In the old days, you would look for somebody who was a talented writer or a talented artist, take them in, and train them in the craft. These days, the economies of the business are such that agencies have less time to train. Happily, and perhaps not so coincidentally, the colleges and the advertising training industry have taken up the slack. So, increasingly, we look for people who have pre-developed portfolios, whether they got them in school, or a series of part-time jobs, or some place like the Portfolio Center, which is essentially a post-graduate school. But that kind of training alone has its own limitations. The expectations it creates can lead to confrontation with real-world experiences. It's like a lawyer who studies Constitutional Law and then ends up working at a big corporate law firm and never touches a constitutional law issue.

Besides, advertising will advance only if people bring more to it than just a knowledge of advertising. It's good if people have a broader education and more unexpected experience. But ultimately, a bright creative mind is still the key.

JAY SCHULBERG
BOZELL WORLDWIDE

Q: *Could we start by establishing a working definition of advertising?*

A: From my point of view, advertising informs and persuades consumers to think about your product or service and, hopefully, to buy it.

Q: *What does successful advertising do?*

A: The first principle of advertising is to sell. Some people in the creative end tend to get that confused. And sometimes creative—in other words, doing good, or outstanding, or fresh, or innovative creative work—gets out of balance with the selling message.

What we want to do is fresh and unexpected work that is also disciplined, effective, and sound. The way that we approach advertising comes down to four or five basic points.

One is to develop a very good strategy with a meaningful selling proposition. Once we have the strategy, the creative work has to be on strategy, and the selling message has to come through. It should be executed in an intrusive way. That can be done with humor or charm or emotion, etc., any of those elements. The humor or the charm or the brilliance must reinforce the selling message.

Finally, the creative must reward the reader for reading and the viewer for watching.

Q: *Could you describe the role that advertising plays in the total buying process?*

A: It informs people and, done well, it informs them persuasively. Most people would not be aware of most products, nor be inclined to buy them, without being informed by advertising that they exist and that they fulfill the need of the consumer.

Let me use an example. Huggies diapers is an enormously successful product. Without advertising, people would just have a random choice from a number of superficially similar products. With advertising, the public is informed that Huggies exist. Taking it one step further, by talking about what the benefit is to the consumer, the consumer is in a better position to understand the less apparent, but not less important, strengths of the product.

For Huggies, the initial strategy or selling promise was that they helped stop leaking. The basic execution was built around the mother's embarrassment, e.g., a christening ceremony and the priest or minister holding the baby and saying "Uh-oh!" to a grandmother holding the baby with the same comment. From an executional point of view, that's cute and it's charming. However, from a strategic point of view, it was wrong, and the brand was performing poorly. What we did when we got the account was fine-tune the strategy and then come up with a unique execution. What is the ultimate benefit? It helps stop leaking to help make *your baby happier.* That's what we changed to. Mothers who buy diapers don't want to admit that they're buying a particular brand due to a selfish motivation such as the mother's embarrassment—the original position in the strategy.

Q: *How do you see television advertising and print advertising as being different and being the same?*

A: They're the same in the sense that all good advertising has to be intrusive, it has to be noticed, it has to be relevant, etc. It has to do all that.

But the mediums do do and can do different things. TV can create awareness more quickly with a larger percentage of the population at a lower cost. To do that in print becomes prohibitively expensive; it's almost impossible. However, print can inform better.

If one has a complicated message or where the consumer is spending a lot of money for a product, such as a car or a VCR or a television set, people want information, and you can get a lot more into print than you can get into a 30-second spot. So, where TV may create the awareness, say for a car, people want to read about what the car has, in my view.

Q: *Do certain types of products or appeals work better in one of the media versus the other?*

A: Yes. There's a general rule of thumb that if you're spending a lot of money for a product—again, a car, a television set, a VCR—you need information. That works better in print. Years ago I wrote an ad for Sears color TV sets, which at the time was the third most expensive item a person bought—you bought a house, a car, and a TV set. I wrote a double-page spread, and it was a thousand words of copy.

The ad was how to buy a color TV from Sears or anyone else. People read it. It was a campaign by itself, and it ran for four years. It was informative. It told people what they had to know about buying a TV set and all that sort of business. It gave them a lot of information. You can't do that in a 30-second spot.

Q: *Could you describe the role of the creative person in creative advertising?*

A: Yes. Creative people have to be all-around advertising people. They're not just art directors and writers who sit in the corners and somebody says, "Go write an ad on Merrill Lynch or Excedrin." They get involved with everything. They get involved with developing the strategy; they have to understand a good selling proposition; they need to know what a smart strategy is. They have to understand all nuances of marketing and be able to monitor change once they create the creative work. No creative work begins until the strategy is identified and fine-tuned.

Q: *Can you describe the difference between a creative commercial and an effective commercial?*

A: Going back years ago, there were the Harry and Bert Piel commercials for Piel's Beer. Everybody loved them—they were charming, they were funny, they were good. Great creative work, but they didn't sell the product; either they lost sight of what their objective was and they didn't know how to fix it, or it was too late to fix it. Today I think examples of good creative work that sells are Jeep and New York Times. They're creative in the sense that they bring the consumer into the advertisement, and once in, they're being sold on the product or service as opposed to just being entertained.

Q: *What is the hardest part about creating a print ad?*

A: One of the problems we have in the business today is that there is a whole generation or two now that has grown up on television and television commercials. There's an allure to commercials that's like making a movie. But with television there are a lot of places to hide. You go out and hire a very expensive director, a very expensive production company, and the film looks great. There are a lot of people who get involved.

With print, there's no place to hide—there's just the writer, the art director, and a blank piece of paper. And that's why it's harder to do print than to do TV. The writer and art director have to sit there and face a blank piece of paper.

Q: *How long does it take to do a print ad?*

A: I don't think there is any set answer. It comes back down to what is the idea. Sometimes you can come up with an idea very quickly. Other times you say, "Oh, my God, I can't think of anything." You walk around and it can be instantaneous or it can take weeks or months, and then you're coupled with a deadline pressure and you have to come up with an idea.

Q: *In terms of the creative challenge, is there a difference between consumer and business-to-business advertising?*

A: I don't believe that there are differences. Actually, a lot of the business-to-business should be just as emotional as consumer advertising. Even though you have to present a lot of information, it still can be done in a charming way, in an engaging way, and in a way which gets people's attention. It does not have to be dry or hack or boring because it is a so-called rational buying decision. By becoming more consumer oriented, more benefit driven, business-to-business advertising is becoming more intrusive, more persuasive, and more emotional.

Q: *Do you have a favorite way to describe the major components of print advertising?*

A: What's important is that it all works together as a unit. The ad itself has to be intrusive, and that can come about in a number of different ways. While the headline or the visual is intrusive, they both have to support one another.

Q: *What is the role of celebrities in print advertising?*

A: Most celebrity advertising in my view is wrong. It works only if the celebrity reinforces the selling message and is on strategy. For example, Bozell created the Milk Mustache campaign featuring celebrities Naomi Campbell, Lauren Bacall, Joan Rivers, Kate Moss, Kristi Yamaguchi, and many, many more.

The purpose of the campaign is educational. Many women need to drink more milk for health reasons.

They are not drinking it for the *wrong* reasons—fat content. The fact is, skim or 1% milk contain all the vitamins, minerals, and calcium as whole milk, without fat or less fat. Many people don't know this. They think all the good stuff is taken out with the fat.

The celebrity with a milk mustache is a grabber that gets people's attention. The ad is almost a poster. There are only a few lines of copy. The opening and closing lines reflect the celebrity's personality. Lines two and three contain a surprising nugget of new information about milk to persuade women to drink. Celebrities in the milk campaign are relevant to specfic target audiences. For example, Kate Moss and Naomi Campbell are targeted to teenagers; Joan Rivers and Lauren Bacall, to older women.

Q: *How about the role of humor in print advertising?*

A: Years ago there used to be a campaign for Dewar's which I thought was terrific. It was humor in advertising; it was as if Tommy Smothers wrote an ad for Dewar's. Other than that, I can think of very few examples of humor in print advertising. Why don't we see more? I don't know the answer. I think it's a fascinating question. Part of it may be that it's hard to keep it fresh. The humor that is there is not a "ha-ha," it's more of a warm type of a thing, the Snoopy and Metropolitan Life campaign, perhaps, or the sophisticated uses in Chivas Regal.

Q: *How do you decide on the size of the ad—one page versus a spread? Is that part of the creative issue?*

A: Yes, and it comes from two things. One is obviously the amount of money the client has to spend and then, beyond that, what is the largest size or the smallest size one can get away with and still be effective. I think one of the things we do wrong in the business is that people don't tend to make judgments on what is the most effective selling unit. One can often get away well with one-quarter page or a one-third page. Both the advertiser and agency can be guilty of a sometimes automatic reaction to go with a full page or spread. It's a temptation that should be resisted.

Q: *When is it time to start a new campaign?*

A: When the old one is not working anymore. One of the fundamental mistakes made in advertising is that campaigns change for the sake of change. That's one of the most destructive things imaginable. It's very hard to come up with a good campaign and a very good campaign that sells. And once you have it, you ought to stick with it and stay with it for years. What you do is try to keep it fresh and evolve it and, as I said, be able to read changes in the marketplace so you make changes and refinements in the executions and the creative work.

Q: *I was wondering if you might be able to describe an example of a campaign that has been consistent over time but has changed also in response to improvements in the product or changes in the marketplace.*

A: What we try to do is maintain the executional equity that we have, that we know is working, but make refinements within it. Let's go back to Huggies as an example, although it's more of a TV account than it is print. We start off with a very simple proposition, and that is, as I said, "it helps stop leaking to make babies happier." And then we did what we believe was a very unique execution within the diapers package goods category. We avoided the typical clichés most advertisers were doing at that time, which was basically having mothers and fathers cooing over babies mouthing copy points. We opted instead for what were basically before-and-after demonstrations.

Some creative people make a mistake, because they refuse to change the advertising because they think it is just great the way it is. Conversely, there is often considerable pressure to throw out the old advertising and start over again because we have something new to say. Our solutions are generally to evolve the advertising. We seek out a way to read the marketplace, read changes in the marketplace, and to incorporate news while still retaining an executional equity.

Q: *You increasingly hear the concept of brand personality or character. Is that a term that applies to what you're describing now?*

A: All advertising has a personality—good or bad, prestige or schlock, meaningful or not. Jeep, for example, stands for individuality. "There's only one Jeep." So you're not going to do something that is out of character. A creative team can come up with a great execution, but if it's out of the tone and manner of the personality of that product or advertiser, it doesn't fly—we reject it.

A lot of it is not very good. On the creative end, we do not have enough people who are interested in creating great print advertising. It's improving, but their first disposition is to go to television. We have to get them away from that. And actually, some of the better people, some of the better agencies coming along today, are building their reputation not on TV but on print. Also, I think that many advertisers think it's okay to have theater, humor, or whatever the case may be, in TV. But in print we're going to tell them the facts. And that's the wrong approach as well. To go back to the basic things again, make it emotional, make it provocative, make it interesting, make it benefit oriented. The same philosophy applies to print. I think all of us have to do better print.

Q: *A number of people have characterized the current direction in advertising as moving from selling to serving and hawking to helping. What trends or directions do you see in print advertising as we look ahead from here?*

A: I think that you will see a trend to do more intrusive print, more unexpected print, more engaging print, and more in print that rewards the reader for reading. You've got to get people's attention; otherwise, it's a total waste of the client's money.

Clients pay to advertise, but no one is paid to read an ad or watch a TV spot. As more and more people begin to flip a page or flip a channel, you have to find ways to get their attention without just shock for the sake of shock.

Q: *What is your favorite myth about advertising that you would like to dispel?*

A: That advertising forces people to buy things that they don't need. I don't believe that. The product can disappoint people, and therefore they won't come back and buy it again. But to say that advertising is an artificial stimulus and forces people to buy things they don't want is really to misunderstand the role of advertising and the individuality of the consumer.

Q: *In the 1950s, Rosser Reeves said that the most dangerous word in all of advertising is "originality." Do you agree or disagree?*

A: I disagree strongly. One has to have originality, and if we did not have originality in advertising or anything else, the world would stop. Progress would stop. We wouldn't be moving forward. We constantly have to be pushing the frontiers and expanding them. And that's what originality is about. You have to be disciplined in the way that you do it.

Originality—mindless originality, or something which is irrelevant or undisciplined—is wrong. But to say that there should be no originality, period, is just as wrong. I think that's one of the things that went wrong in the seventies. It makes people slaves to the past and the formulas and the rules, and when that happens, progress stops. So one must have originality.

Q: *What advice do you have for new people coming into the industry?*

A: The same advice somebody gave me when I was starting out—he said, "work twice as hard as the next guy."

Q: *What is your most inviolate rule in creating print advertising, and when should it be violated?*

A: The rule is very simple, as I said in the beginning— brilliant, unexpected creative that sells brilliantly. This should never be violated.

BOB SKOLLAR
GREY ADVERTISING

Q: *Bob, let's start with a definition of what advertising is.*

A: Strange animal. It's really a combination of art, science, and business. Advertising tells people something about a product or service and gives them some reason to say, "I'll try it. I'll try it once." After that, it's really the product performance that sells them. Advertising should provide that one little thing that helps people say, "I'm interested. I'll give it a shot."

Q: *How does advertising contribute to the purchase process?*

A: It's part of the mix. I am not a big believer in immediate persuasion—how, after seeing a commercial, a person says "That's it. I'm going out and buying the product right now." Sometimes when you hit it right it works like that, but usually a decision to purchase results from a combination of things in the whole marketplace. You start with the product. You have to have a valid product proposition. I like to think about it as a "telephone fact." What would you tell someone on the telephone about the product? What would be the reason you would give them to go buy it? That's about how much time we have, and it's one of the keys to successful advertising. You want to say something that's relevant to the person—that the person looks at and says, "Yeah, that's something that could work for me."

Q: *Let's turn it around a little bit. Why do you think people look at advertising? What do you think they're trying to get out of it?*

A: In addition to being entertaining—that's how you get someone to look at it—we have to offer up something that people want to know about. Now, sometimes what they want to "know" is an image. More often than not, what they want to know is a fact or factor that is going to affect the way they live in some way. They're looking to get some information—to find out more about what's out in the marketplace—new product, better product. *Why* they look at this particular ad gets into the crafting of it. How do we get their interest? First, you have to get them to look at it. I don't think most people start out by saying, "All right, I want to find out something about a product. Let me go through this magazine to see if I can find this information. I know I have to put up with the articles, but let me see if I can get some advertising information from this magazine." The ad has to grab them and say, "Listen. We've got something important or something interesting to tell you or something you may want to know about." There is no one way to do that. That's where the art takes over. Grab someone's attention, whether it's print or television, hold them for a few seconds, and get your message out there quickly and clearly.

Q: *How do you know if advertising is successful?*

A: The main measure I'm concerned about is sales in the marketplace, and even that can be iffy. Like I said, the best we can do is get people to try it once. For example, I've worked on Domino's Pizza. Like all restaurants, Domino's comes out with a lot of new products. We can do an ad and say, "Now we have buffalo wings," and get them to try it once, but if they are not good, they're not going to try them again. So it can be very hard to determine ad effectiveness. There are times when we're on air and times when we're off air, and sometimes you notice when you're on air that sales are really going up. That tells you something.

Advertising can't take all the credit, but there is something going on there, whether it's awareness or whether there's something motivating people to cause them to do something. One of the interesting things about retail advertising is that you can know the next day if you have to fill up seats in a restaurant or if you have to get orders in a restaurant; you *know* if it's working or not. We also do research. We read the tracking data, and we get some awareness of that advertising and hear what people say about it. Often we test the ad in focus groups. But we also do something more quantitative. You look at numbers and you say, "Well, gee, a norm is 21 and this got a 24." Does that mean it's going to be successful in the marketplace? No. It gives you some guideline that says people are "getting it," whether they understand what the message is. Research can be a terrific creative tool. It's great for discovering real language, and people will tell you if you're off or not. They may say, "I don't

believe that a second." It can be tough for a creative guy to hear, but you can learn if you're onto the right thing or in the right direction.

Q: *Do you have a case history you can share that demonstrates the value of advertising?*

A: Kool-Aid. Kool-Aid is a product that's popular with kids, but it competes against some tough competitors, like colas and other soft drinks. Kids like Kool-Aid, but there is "something" about Pepsi and Coke; they had Madonna and all the celebrities and, of course, your Mom and Dad drink it. So Kool-Aid had this nice little niche—a kid's drink—and we set out to see if we could even boost this up a little bit more through advertising. We created a campaign that tried to own its own type of cool—not a Pepsi cool but a kids kind of cool—and did the advertising over a couple years. Then a few years back we did a tracking study, and we asked the question, "Which is the coolest drink? All of a sudden we saw that Kool-Aid, for the 6–12 age group, moved ahead of Coke and Pepsi. Now, I can't say it's all because of the advertising, but it shows that advertising certainly helps.

Q: *Turning to print, what's print for? What does it do?*

A: First, let me tell you how I feel about print. I love print, and the reason I love it is because there's no "cheating." It goes straight to the heart of the matter. In television you use great background music, do a great special effect, and get one of those terrific directors, and even the ugliest idea can become beautiful. In print, there is no hiding. You have to have it in basically a headline and a visual image. Either you have an idea or you don't. Now, of course, you can get beautiful photography, show a beautiful girl, you show a cute little baby, but it still turns on the quality of the idea. Another thing about print advertising is that it comes with the ultimate remote control. You're "flicking" those pages, you're usually not looking for the advertising. I've got to grab you on that one page. The other thing is that print is really the best writer's challenge. It's about writing. It's about language. It's about words much more so than television. Television used to be like a print ad that goes on for 30 seconds, but it's become much more visual and image oriented. In print, though, whether you use one word or long copy to get your message across, it really is very much about crafting language. Print is also used when you have limited budgets, when you want to convey information about a product, or when you're trying to hit certain types of people. For example, you can reach working women a lot easier with women's magazines than with television.

Q: *Can you convey mood and emotion in print?*

A: I think you can. Look at a photograph, go to any museum, you can get emotion from what you see. There's no reason why you cannot get it from a print ad. And words, too. You get words in there that hit you right in the heart or the soul. Putting a quote from a child that creates a picture in the reader's mind is an emotional experience. It's a challenge. You don't have music or the sweeping shots of television to help you out.

Q: *If you have a campaign that includes both print and TV, how do you like to think about the two media working?*

A: They have to work together. Whatever a client does, whatever product we're working on, we're better off when we speak with one voice and have basically one message. We don't want to be unclear or confusing. Now that doesn't mean it has to be identical: a couple of clips from TV with a headline to it. But it has to be coming from the same sensibility. We think a lot about brand character, which is the way that the brand is perceived over years. It's everything other than the facts about the brand. What is my feeling about the brand, who is the brand? When I look at a print ad and I see a TV commercial, if I see they're talking about two different brand characters, I would never recommend that. Just as if I was doing four television commercials, I don't think they have to be "cookie cutters," but I think there are basic core sensibilities and message components that have to exist across the campaign. I want you to hear one voice essentially.

Q: *How does the audience to which the advertising is targeted play into what the advertiser says or shows?*

A: It's critical. That's where you have to start. We can't do advertising for ourselves. You have to have a real sensibility about who our audiences are. Go and talk to them. Do groups. Talk to people before we do the advertising. Hear what they say about it and what's important to them. I do a lot of kids' advertising. I think I'm able to do it pretty well, because I love being around kids. But it's very important that I avoid sitting around in a room with a group of executives saying, "Oh, kids will really like this." We do a lot of testing with kids. We show them print ads and storyboards. They will tell you very much if you've got it and will help you make it better. I'm talking about kids now, but the point is relevant to anybody. You have to know

your audience. Some creative people say they're trying to do "cool" advertising. I like cool advertising. Sometimes cool advertising is the right thing to do, but sometimes it's not. It depends on who you're talking to, what is their frame of mind. If you're talking about something that's real important to them, If you're talking to a mom, if you're talking to someone who's making an important decision right away, "cool" is not necessarily the motivating word. It's understanding. You're trying to get inside the head of the consumer—trying to say something that is very relevant to them. To me, you always want their heads going up and down before you hit them with the facts. Is this your life? Is this what's important to you? Is this something you've been talking about? If the head is going up and down, you say, "Well, let me tell you something." If they say, "That's not me" or "They're not talking to me," if you don't nail your consumer right and not just demographically—really psychographically and understand what the head is about—the most fun advertising in the world, even advertising that wins all the awards, is not gonna really work.

Q: *Is advertising becoming more targeted to the different psychographic groups, or does it still search for mass appeals?*

A: Well, there are a couple answers. Certainly, there are a couple of reasons for saying it's becoming more targeted. One, media capabilities, both with print and television, allow you to slice the pie very thin. And it seems there are new magazines coming out every week that are very, very targeted. The other point is products. There are more and more products out there, and every one's looking for its little niche. It's a totally different world than it was even five years ago. There are so many new products out there. Many are going after the same mass, but some are starting to focus a little more and trying to grab a particular group. The flip side of it is that there are a lot of clients whose budgets are down. Sometimes we do three campaigns—one for the kid group and one for the teen group and one for the adult group. Sometimes we've got to get a message that appeals to everybody.

Q: *One often hears about rational versus emotional types of appeals or feature/benefit versus image kinds of advertising. What do these terms mean to you and are they relevant distinctions at this point?*

A: They sound like they're different, but to me, the best advertising is a combination of both. I'll go back to my "telephone facts." If you've told me a fact that's important that I haven't heard before, we are pretty much there. Give it to me in the "right envelope," and I may be willing to watch the commercial or read the print ad. But most of the time you don't really have this huge product difference, and then it's a matter of positioning for image advertising or emotional advertising. You want to combine them both, and if you don't really have that rational point, you look for something that at least is conveyed differently so that the consumer sees that there is a distinctive difference in this product. And then there is how you *feel* about the product, which can be as important as the rational fact behind the product. When you get into certain areas like a perfume or things like that, "rational" is a very small part, but positioning is very important. But image and emotion are not just a bunch of pretty pictures. It helps a person say, "I know where this goes in my world."

Q: *Could you describe the process that you go through to create a print ad?*

A: For me, there is no one method. Every person works differently, and I believe in whatever works. I don't sit down and say, "Now I have to come up with a print ad." I have the assignment and I start thinking about it. And I work that way until the whistle blows and I have to turn something in to the client. I do that with television and I do that with print. I like to think about it and talk about it, and I may write something down as I first wake in the morning. I jot something down on a piece of paper, or I may not be thinking about it at the time—you know, I'm doing something with my child, and I see an image. That's a great image, and I say, "You know what. I'm going to file that someplace, because that works very well for what I've been thinking about here." And rarely am I only thinking about one thing.

Structurally, we work as teams, and each art director and writer have their own method of working, but there's a time when you close the door and you start throwing around ideas. I don't like the hard distinction between writers and art directors. To me, a good writer has to think more about an ad than its words and a good art director has to think of some kind of message, words that communicate.

Q: *You mentioned that you start with the assignment. What are the inputs that you start with?*

A: I think most good creatives like the creative part of the process *and* the business part of it. I resent being handed the strategy. It used to be that a writer gave an art director a script—here it is, go draw the pictures. I feel kind of the same way when a strategy is slipped

under the door. I work better when involved very, very early. When someone has a new product coming out, I want to talk about it. Talk about it not in terms of let's start throwing out some advertising, but what is it about, what we were saying before, where is the consumer on this? Unfortunately, we don't do as much of this as we would like. But it works better when we know more about the competitive frame, the way people are using the product now, and what they think about it, if there is any kind of personality going on, if they think about other than the rational side of it before we start doing the advertising. I like creative people to get involved very, very early in the process, before the assignment is handed out, and then once they have it, have enough time to really think about it.

Q: *When you judge a piece of print advertising, what do you look for? Do you look at the ad as a whole or look at the pieces? What do you think about the headline, the illustration, the body copy, and identification?*

A: Anytime someone comes to me with advertising, I don't look at the advertising first. I say, "Tell me what the idea is." I want to make sure of the idea. If they say, "We have this cute little kid sitting on a swing," I say, "That's the execution. Tell me about the idea. What are you trying to say?" Then I look at the ad not as an advertising guy, but (as much as I can sitting in this office) I try to see myself as someone on a train reading a magazine. Am I gonna look at it? And if I look at it, what do I think or feel?

I don't think that any two people look at an ad in the same way. If there's a very stopping graphic, then that's where my eyes are going to go. If it's a big headline, if it's something that's going to grab my attention, that's where my eyes are going to go. If it's the product, if it's the person—I'm not big on rules, except to make sure you have a focus on the idea and make sure that it's compelling enough so that people can become involved with it quickly.

Q: *Some people think that it's getting harder and harder for ads to get noticed, for people to get involved with them. Do you think this is true, and what are some of the things in terms of print you can use to make advertising more compelling or more involved?*

A: There's so much stuff out there that people are bombarded every place they look. This makes it harder to break through. Everybody knows that. That's a cliche. But there are things that help counter this trend. New technology in photography and broadcasting gives us more tools to use to make advertising more interesting. And while there are always people that knock advertising, when you do entertaining advertising, people like it and will look at it. I said it's becoming a little part of our culture. Advertising is a good information vehicle, but people don't go out looking for advertising to get information. But when it's there—when it grabs you—you say, "Oh good, I didn't know that before. I like that. I'll remember this when I'm in a store or I will ask a friend about it."

Q: *You mentioned some of the new technology. On the print side, at least, how is the computer changing how ads are created?*

A: I remember the first time one of our new art directors brought me an ad that he did on a computer. I was floored. What used to take weeks and had to be sent out could now be done in hours! But it's also a double-edged sword. Art direction can too easily become "What can I do on my computer?" So, what I've been doing lately is going back a little to the old days. I ask my art directors to bring me in the napkin with the idea on it. Bring me the image that you want to do. I get nervous when someone begins thinking about an idea in terms of how to do it on the computer. It's great that you can go in and make an idea come to life a little bit, but it can't limit our creativity.

Q: *How do you know when an ad's become stale and when it's time for something new?*

A: That usually comes from our research people or from our account side. There are some things people like looking at over and over again, and some that have less a "shelf life" than others.

Q: *There are certain devices that sometimes people use in print advertising to try to get more attention or more involvement, things like celebrities or coupons. How do you think about those kinds of devices, and do they have a role in creative advertising?*

A: I don't like to think about them as devices, and they are two different things. Let's start with coupons, because that's easy. If you've got a coupon for something, you use it. You need that call to action and, to me, the coupon is the ultimate call to action. We're always trying to build it into our advertising somehow. There are some people who will try the product now because of the coupon and others who will feel better about the product because of the coupon—both are "win situations."

Q: *Are coupons usually part of the assignment or do they come out of the creation of the ad?*

A: They're part of the assignment, because that's a company decision. Celebrities? Celebrities are good if you have an idea first. I'm sure you can take an ad, throw in a celebrity's face, and probably get a little more awareness or recognition, but I don't think that's the way to use them. It should be a question of "What am I trying to say? There's a person out there who stands for that, who says that, who will make people think about that a lot quicker."

Q: *What advice do you have for people who are trying to get into the business, particularly on the creative side? What kind of training do you think they should have? What kind of abilities do you look for, and how should they go about developing their skills?*

A: A lot of the schools now teach how to *think* about advertising and are very good at it. But what's most important is that you really have to like advertising. When I hire someone, whether it's junior or not, you can tell right away if they like it. If you want to be an artist, you should be an artist. There's plenty of room to do artistic things in advertising, but it is a very, very cooperative effort. You have to have strong enough ideas so that when people start chipping away at them, and it's going to happen I guarantee you with any account, you've got to bend but not break. The other thing is for writers. You've got to like writing. It's not about "Gee, I got a quick, cool idea." It's very hard to get away with that anymore, especially when you're starting out, because very often you're not the one who's up for the next big campaign. Finally, print is a great way to do your spec book. If you can do it in print, you can probably do it in TV. And when they're doing a spec for a print ad, write body copy. I want to see if you like language. Do you know how to write conversationally? Do you have a flow of writing? Do you play with words? Most of all you'll need the passion. You gotta love it!

NOTE

Preceding editions of *Which Ad Pulled Best?* have concentrated on what might be called "general" advertising—magazine advertisements appearing in big-circulation consumer magazines or business magazines.

But in the last few years, "Direct Response" advertising has exploded as the fastest-growing type of advertising. Many general advertisers could profit from observing successful direct response techniques, and vice-versa.

Accordingly, for this edition we have added the following pages containing an interview with a successful user of direct response advertising. In these pages he defines the medium, describes some of its techniques, and points out how it differs from or is like general advertising.

ANDREW JOSEPH BYRNE
Consultant in Direct Marketing and Direct Advertising

Q: *The most popular advertising medium for direct marketers is direct mail. Do you have any "dos" and "don'ts" on direct mail?*

A: Yes. After you decide what you're going to say in a direct mailing, you answer the question, "Who's going to receive it?" So you're talking about mailing lists. And if you're making a mailing that actually *sells* a product or service by mail, you're wise to use "response" lists. These are mailing lists of people who have *bought* something by mail.

The other big mailing list category is "compiled" lists. These names have been taken from sources as directories and membership lists. Telephone owners and car owners are examples of large compiled mailing lists.

Surprisingly, even though a compiled list has demographics and psychographics very similar to those of your customers, it will practically never be as effective as a response list.

If your mailing isn't actually selling something by mail, that's when compiled lists make sense. You may, for example, need to obtain sales leads for sales people. And enough of these sales leads must come in from particular territories. Response lists will practically never have enough names in concentrated territories. Instead, they're spread out. So, compiled mailing lists are the answer.

Now, here's a point that surprises people about direct mailings. The letter is the most important part of the mailing. I'm talking about a sales letter which should be used, not a weak "cover" letter which introduces the brochure. They are abominations.

The importance of the letter is a surprise to people, because the brochure might be four to six times more expensive. One explanation is that, while the brochure is "advertising" to the prospect, the letter is envisioned as a message from its signer, even though the same copywriter probably wrote both.

There have been tests made of a mailing that included a letter, a brochure, and a reply device. 50 percent of a mailing list received the brochure and reply device. The other 50 percent received the letter and reply device. The "letter" mailing won.

Incidentally, if the letter reads just like the brochure, it's a lousy letter. It should be one person talking to one other person. The "our's" and "we's" should be thrown out. There should be plenty of "you's" and "your's" and a sprinkling of "I's" and "me's," just as there would be in a regular letter a person would write. Again, one person talking to one other person.

Q: *How about a couple of "dos."*

A: Okay. Here are a couple. Do prove your claim whenever you make one. Everyone makes claims. But your statements are believed only if you prove they are true. Support your claims with facts and figures. Use testimonials and case histories. Offer guarantees. And remember this: words like, "quality," "value," "service," and "dependability" aren't proof of anything.

Here's another "do." Do document the need for your product. Again, do use case histories, facts on the problem your product solves. Even though you may have proved your product is better than a competitor's, if the reader hasn't been shown that there's a problem, why should he be interested in your solution?

Q: *A final question. Any recommendations on writing style?*

A: Yes. Keep it simple, clear, and direct—short words, short sentences, short paragraphs. But I didn't say short copy.

Douglas Mueller of Gunning-Mueller Clear Writing Institute makes a great point. He reminds us that the *Wall Street Journal* covers complex subjects in language clearly understood by a junior in high school. Except for the front page. It's written to be understood by a freshman in high school. Other publications like *Newsweek* and *U.S. News* use identical standards.

Why so simple? Because research proved that the simpler the writing, the *more* would be read by their sophisticated, well-educated readers.

About 145 years ago, Nathaniel Hawthorne wrote this to an editor: "The greatest possible merit of style is, of course, to make the words absolutely disappear into the thought."

New York advertising executive Lois Korey observed, "The best print advertising seems to the reader to have no style. It's simply an intelligent, believable presentation of the facts."

The following 40 sets
of Consumer Advertisements
were tested by Gallup & Robinson

EXAMPLE 1

A

Take it personally.

And take your hair beyond beautiful. To salon beautiful. With Salon Selectives personalized shampoos 1, 3, 4, 5, 6, 7 and conditioners B, H, S, P, F, M. Choose the combination perfectly right. Just for you. Isn't it wonderful to feel like you just stepped out of a salon?

B

When we introduced our Australian 3 Minute Miracle® Reconstructor and Conditioner in 1979, we felt it was one of the best deep conditioners you could buy. We still think so. And, it continues to be one of our most popular products. Originally developed for the salon, Australian 3 Minute Miracle has ingredients that:

- smooth rough cuticle layers
- increase shine by making hair more reflective to light
- penetrate to reconstruct damaged hair, inside & out

Just one 3-minute treatment will restore moisture, manageability and shine . . . and convince you that this is one product that lives up to its name!

We'll never compromise on ingredients. We'll never skimp on quality.

EXAMPLE 1

CONSUMER

Background.   These full-page advertisements appeared in *People* magazine. Ad A ran in February, and Ad B in April of the following year. *People* focuses on compelling personalities of our time, from the known to the unknown, the famous to the infamous, the ordinary to the extraordinary. Likewise, the publication serves as a guide to important developments in the arts, sciences, politics, sports, television, motion pictures, books, and records, with the spotlight on people involved in those areas. Which of these advertisements do you think obtained the higher Gallup & Robinson scores among women readers?

STUDENT ANALYSIS

NAME _____ CLASS _____ DATE _____

EXAMPLE 2

A

"What's the best way to face skin that's changing? Change your make up. I did."
—Christine Brinkley

"That's why my make-up is Replenishing Make-up from Cover Girl. Its line-diminishing coverage is so natural. Even more, it renews the look and feel of skin that's changing, like mine. I give its hydro-replenishers all the credit. They help prevent little lines. And help my skin look more radiant. Even a little younger. You'll see, it's a beautiful way to face the future!"

B

With skin like hers ask her age and automatically she subtracts 5 years. Who does she think she's fooling?

Everyone.

New Maybelline Revitalizing™. The Age-Denying Make-up.

Light-reflecting coverage diffuses fine lines

SPF 10 helps protect skin.

Vitamin A and moisturizers.

Revitalizes for a younger look. Even up close.

EXAMPLE 2

CONSUMER

Background. Both of these were full-page advertisements. Ad A appeared in the *Ladies' Home Journal* in March, and Ad B appeared in December of the preceding year in *Harper's Bazaar*. *Ladies' Home Journal* contains features and articles that cover a variety of special interests, including beauty and fashion, food and nutrition, health and medicine, and home decorating and design. *Harper's Ba-zaar* stresses comprehensive coverage of fashion and beauty. It's edited for the discerning woman, with information on the best for home, travel, and food, and also news on entertainment and the arts, health, fitness, and finance. Which of these advertisements do you think obtained higher Gallup & Robinson scores among women readers?

STUDENT ANALYSIS

NAME _____ CLASS _____ DATE _____

EXAMPLE 3

A

We admit it's not standard operating procedure at the major hotel chains. But then Preferred Hotels® and Resorts Worldwide is not a hotel chain.

We're an association of independent hotels.

It's our job to set and maintain the highest possible standards for a group of the finest hotels and resorts around the world. We're very strict when it comes to our standards. And very unforgiving with member hotels and resorts that don't adhere to them.

Admittedly, this is not an attractive concept to the great majority of hotels.

In fact, it's enough to keep all but the very best from applying. Which perhaps explains why, in a world of more than 300,000 hotels and resorts, at present only 105 are Preferred. They represent the very finest accommodations available anywhere at any price.

Interestingly, they are not necessarily the most expensive hotels in their market.

Ask your travel agent if there's a Preferred hotel where you plan to visit.

Or if you would like a directory listing our 105 current members, please call us at 1-800-447-5773.

B

"There are a million things we could do here, and you're just sitting there."

"I know exactly what I want to do next."

EXAMPLE **3**

CONSUMER

Background. *Bon Appétit* magazine carried both of these full-page advertisements, with Ad A running in September and Ad B appearing in May of the preceding year. *Bon Appétit* focuses on sophisticated home entertaining, with emphasis on food and its preparation. Features are included on travel, restaurants, fine tableware, and kitchen design. Regular departments cover new tableware and products; food related collectibles; health and nutrition; quick recipes for weekday meals and entertaining; cooking techniques; wine and spirits; and recipes from restaurants, hotels, and inns around the world. Which of these advertisements to do you think obtained higher Gallup & Robinson scores among women readers?

STUDENT ANALYSIS

NAME _____ CLASS _____ DATE _____

EXAMPLE **4**

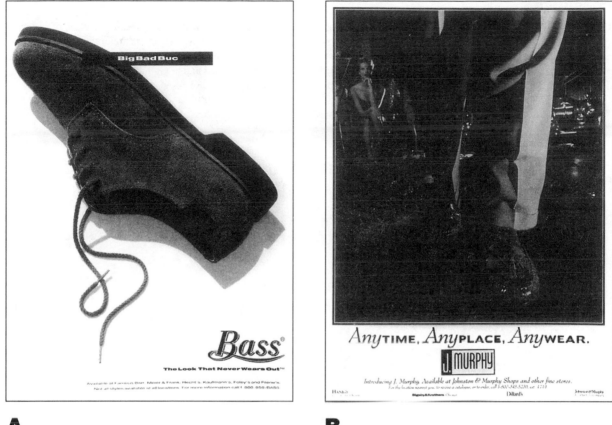

A

Big Bad Buc

Bass. The Look That Never Wears Out.

B

Anytime, Anyplace, Anywear.

EXAMPLE 4

CONSUMER

Background. *Sports Illustrated* carried both of these full-page advertisements. Ad A ran in October and Ad B appeared in June of the following year. *Sports Illustrated* covers the world of sports, which it interprets and follows in depth. Major games and events are presented, with much comment on individuals in sports and the place of sports in contemporary life. Articles on fashion, physical fitness, and conservation are included. Which of these advertisements do you think obtained higher Gallup & Robinson scores among men readers?

STUDENT ANALYSIS

NAME _____ CLASS _____ DATE _____

EXAMPLE **5**

A

Max Factor Diamond Hard Nail Enamel

Finally. Long-lasting-color, nailed.

It's that multi-polymer formula that makes it so durable. And the choice of 55 brilliant shades, that makes it so beautiful.

What's she wearing? Diamond Hard Nail Enamel in Firebrand.

B

Together their advanced Glyoxal formulas give you unbeatably beautiful nails.

Something amazing begins the moment you combine the remarkable advanced Glyoxal formulas of these two nail care breakthroughs. Immediately, their nail fortifying formulas start to condition and protect. Promoting strong, healthy nail growth. Extending nail color wear for days longer.

EXAMPLE 5

CONSUMER

Background. *People* magazine, carrying Ad A, a full-page advertisement focused on compelling personalities in all fields, from the known to the unknown, the famous to the infamous, the ordinary to the extraordinary. *People* serves as a guide to what is important in the arts, sciences, business, politics, television, motion pictures, books and records, and sports, all within the context of the personalities involved. Ad B ran in *Cosmopolitan* as a full page in February, whereas Ad A ran in *People* several years later. *Cosmopolitan* is edited for young women of today, dealing with the emotional side of their lives. Articles include such issues as relationships, careers, science, money, travel, fashion, beauty, food, and decorating. Also, there are celebrity profiles and fiction. Which of these advertisements do you think obtained higher Gallup & Robinson scores among women readers?

STUDENT ANALYSIS

NAME _____ CLASS _____ DATE _____

EXAMPLE **6**

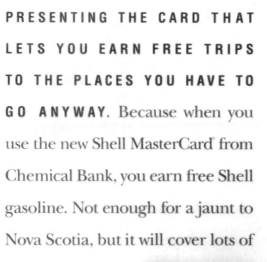

PRESENTING THE CARD THAT LETS YOU EARN FREE TRIPS TO THE PLACES YOU HAVE TO GO ANYWAY. Because when you use the new Shell MasterCard from Chemical Bank, you earn free Shell gasoline. Not enough for a jaunt to Nova Scotia, but it will cover lots of round-trips to work. To apply, just call 1-800-FREE GAS.

A

Presenting the card that lets you earn free trips to the places you have to go anyway.

Because when you use the new Shell MasterCard® from Chemical Bank, you earn free Shell gasoline. Not enough for a jaunt to Nova Scotia, but it will cover lots of round trips to work. To apply, just call 1-800-FREE-GAS.

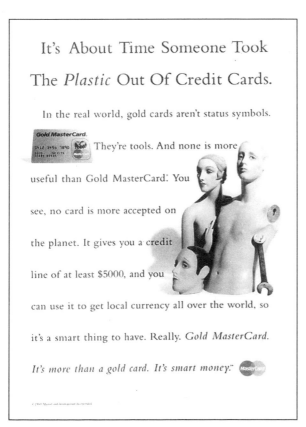

It's About Time Someone Took The *Plastic* Out Of Credit Cards.

In the real world, gold cards aren't status symbols.  They're tools. And none is more useful than Gold MasterCard. You see, no card is more accepted on the planet. It gives you a credit line of at least $5000, and you can use it to get local currency all over the world, so it's a smart thing to have. Really. *Gold MasterCard.*

It's more than a gold card. It's smart money.

B

In the real world, gold cards aren't status symbols. They're tools. And none is more useful than Gold MasterCard®. You see, no card is more accepted on the planet. It gives you a credit line of at least $5000, and you can use it to get local currency all over the world, so it's a smart thing to have. Really. *Gold MasterCard*. It's more than a gold card. It's smart money.

EXAMPLE 6

CONSUMER

Background. Each of these advertisements is a full page. Ad A ran in December, while Ad B ran in November of the following year. *Time* magazine carried Ad A. This publication covers national and world affairs, business news, lifestyles, entertainment news, and reviews. Issues contain photography, charts, and maps. Ad B appeared in *News-week*, another news magazine that reports world and national news and trends in politics, the economy, personal business, the Washington scene, the arts, lifestyles, health, science, and technology. Like *Time*, it offers analysis and commentary. Which of these advertisements to do you think obtained higher Gallup & Robinson scores among men readers?

STUDENT ANALYSIS

NAME _____ CLASS _____ DATE _____

EXAMPLE 7

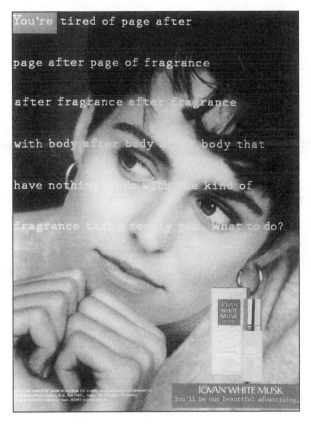

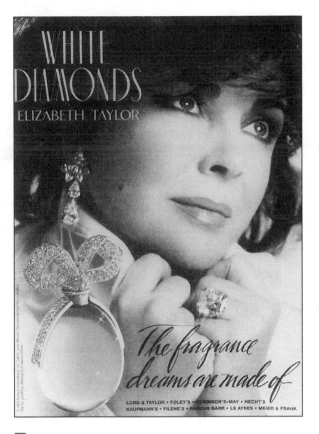

 A

You're tired of page after page of fragrance after fragrance after fragrance with body after body after body that have nothing to do with the kind of fragrance that's really you. What to do?

B

White Diamonds

Elizabeth Taylor

The fragrance dreams are made of.

EXAMPLE 7

CONSUMER

Background. Ad A, a full page, ran in the *Ladies' Home Journal* in November, and Ad B appeared in *People* in October of the following year. *Ladies' Home Journal* contains features and articles about beauty, fashion, food and nutrition, health and medicine, home decorating and design, personalities, and current events. *People* focuses on personalities in all fields, from unknown to famous, ordinary to unusual, and serves as a guide to personalities currently in the limelight in the arts, sciences, business, motion pictures, television, politics, books, records, and sports. Which of these advertisements do you think obtained higher Gallup & Robinson scores among women readers?

STUDENT ANALYSIS

NAME _____ CLASS _____ DATE _____

EXAMPLE 8

A

Experience color so rich you can feel it.

Cover Girl creates remarkable lipcolor.

A distinctly different kind of color. With more richness to the look. More depth to the coverage. More color to the color. The result of an enriched micro-concentrate formula with Vitamin E. For color so luxurious, so rich you can feel it.

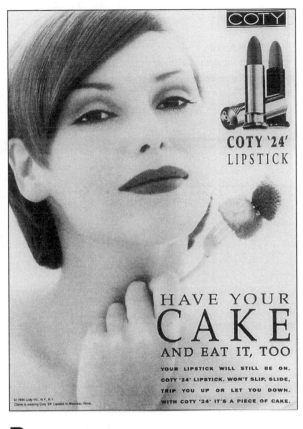

B

Have your cake and eat it, too.

Your lipstick will still be on. Coty '24' lipstick. Won't slip, slide, trip you up or let you down. With Coty '24' it's a piece of cake.

EXAMPLE 8

CONSUMER

Background. *Ladies' Home Journal* ran Ad A in two places in February and September of the same year. Ad B appeared in *Mademoiselle* in February of the preceding year. Both advertisements were full page. *Ladies' Home Journal* contains features and articles that cover a variety of special interests, such as beauty and fashion, food and nutrition, health and medicine, and home decorating and design. *Mademoiselle* is edited for style-conscious women in their twenties. Each issue offers views on fashion, careers, beauty, relationships, health, fitness, entertainment, and social issues. Which of these advertisements do you think obtained higher Gallup & Robinson scores among women readers?

STUDENT ANALYSIS

NAME _____ CLASS _____ DATE _____

EXAMPLE **9**

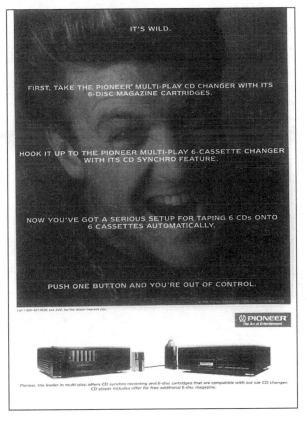

A

1. A $200 trade-in allowance on the Bose® Lifestyle® music system.

New Bose patented technology, including Acoustimass speaker technology and automatic dynamic equalization, has enabled us to reduce the size and complexity of the stereo system while actually improving performance.

This award-winning Lifestyle® music system replaces an entire rack of conventional equipment and speakers.

And now, for a limited time, our participating dealers nationwide will give you at least $200 as a trade in for your stereo system—regardless of size, age, or condition—when you trade up to a Lifestyle® music system.

"No visible speakers, no stack of components, nothing that looks like sound equipment . . . Hit the start button and suddenly the room fills with music of exemplary clarity and fullness."
—Hans Fantel, *The New York Times*, 1990

2. Free speakers from Bose.

During this special event, when you trade up to a Lifestyle® music system, Bose will send you a pair of Lifestyle® powered speakers, a $300 value, free. Now you can add quality sound to your video system, or to a second room, at absolutely no cost.

Bose dealers are also offering a generous trade-in allowance on the new Virtually Invisible® Acoustimass-5 Series II speaker system.

These offers (total values up to $500) end March 31, 1992. For the names of Bose dealers near you, call toll-free: 1-800-444-BOSE Ext. 97.

B

It's wild.

First, take the Pioneer® multi-play CD changer with its 6-disc magazine cartridges.

Hook it up to the Pioneer multi-play 6-cassette changer with its CD syncro feature.

Now you've got a serious setup for taping 6 CDS onto 6 cassettes automatically.

Push one button and you're out of control.

EXAMPLE 9

CONSUMER

Background. Ad A ran in *Business Week* in March; Ad B appeared in *Sports Illustrated* in February of the same year. A management publication, *Business Week* reports ideas and trends affecting the economy or an industry. Material in the magazine provides insights helpful to business executives in the operation of their businesses. Included in the areas covered are finance, technology, media, marketing, government relations, science, labor, social issues, and information processing. *Sports Illustrated* covers the world of sports, including major games and events and individual performers. There is much interpretation and conveying of the character and spirit of sports. Among the articles included are those on physical fitness, conservation, fashion, and the place of sports in contemporary life. Both Ad A and Ad B were full pages. Which of these advertisements do you think obtained higher Gallup & Robinson scores among men readers?

STUDENT ANALYSIS

NAME _____ CLASS _____ DATE _____

EXAMPLE 10

A

At Hyatt, we know just because you've left the office doesn't mean you've left work. Which is why we offer Hyatt Business Centers and Services. Where you can get everything you need—like typing and copying services, computer hook-ups and fax machines. Right where you need them. And the nice thing is, it doesn't matter what you wear to work. To find out all the details about Hyatt Business Centers and Services, call your travel planner or Hyatt at 1-800-233-1234.

B

Why be hampered by the confines of a single hotel room?

When you can be pampered at Marriott Suites. For about the same price.

We'll pamper you with a comfortable bedroom, and a generously appointed living room, as well. So you'll have all the space you need. To work, to conduct meetings, or just relax.

We'll also pamper you with Marriott's warm, attentive service.

And, of course, you'll be receiving Marriott Honored Guest Awards.

So come to Marriott Suites, and let us pamper you.

After all, who deserves it more than you?

EXAMPLE 10

CONSUMER

Background. *Time*, the magazine in which Ad A appeared, covers breaking news, national and world affairs, business news, lifestyles, culture and entertainment news, and reviews. Featured also are photography, charts, and maps. Ad A ran in a December issue. Four years earlier, Ad B appeared in *Newsweek*, which reports weekly developments of world and national news. *Newsweek* contains much analysis and commentary. It considers politics, the economy, personal business, the Washington scene, current affairs, lifestyles, the arts, health, science, and technology. Both ads were full pages. Which of these advertisements do you think obtained higher Gallup & Robinson scores among men readers?

STUDENT ANALYSIS

NAME _____ CLASS _____ DATE _____

EXAMPLE 11

Has something come between you and your skin care?

PURPOSE from Johnson&Johnson

A

Nurse him at 3 am, get up and go to work, don't talk to me about a 5-step beauty plan. I don't have time.

Here at last is PURPOSE® Dual Treatment Moisturizer from Johnson & Johnson—the one, simple way to soft skin. It's wonderfully light, it won't clog your pores, it has no fragrance, it has just the right sunscreen, dermatologists love it.

Take 15 seconds and put it on. You're beautiful. Tired, but beautiful.

Kiss the baby for us.

Have a life. And have beautiful skin, too.

B

Discover Eye Defense Gel-Cream with Liposomes

Created by the Skincare Laboratories of L'Oreál, Eye Defense combines the lightness of a gel and effectiveness of a cream to bring extraordinary tri-action defense to your delicate eye area, where the signs of aging first appear.

Action 1: Smoothes lines and wrinkles.

Action 2: Reduces puffiness.

Action 3: Helps diminish dark circles.

Plénitude Eye Defense. Now reduce the visible effects of aging around your eyes.

EXAMPLE 11

CONSUMER

Background. Ad A appeared in an August issue of *Self* magazine. *Self* is edited for active, professional women who are interested in improving the quality of their lives and the world they live in. The magazine provides a balanced approach to attaining individual satisfaction, with information on beauty, health, fitness, food, fashion, culture, career, politics, and the environment. Ad B ran in February of the same year in *Ladies' Home Journal*. This publication addresses a variety of special interests, including beauty and fashion, food and nutrition, health and medicine, home decorating and design, parenting and self help, personalities, and current events. Both Ad A and Ad B were run as full-page advertisements. Which of these advertisements do you think obtained higher Gallup & Robinson scores among women readers?

STUDENT ANALYSIS

NAME _____ CLASS _____ DATE _____

EXAMPLE **12**

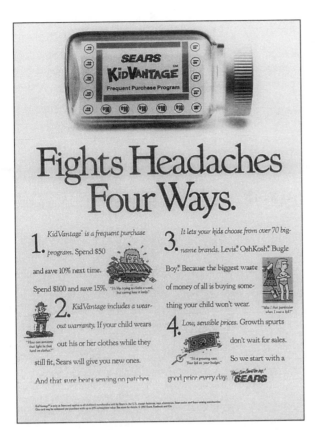

A

1. *KidVantage^{TM} is a frequent purchase program*. Spend $50 and save 10% next time. Spend $100 and save 15%.

"It's like trying to do clothe a weed, but caring how it looks."

2. *KidVantage includes a wear-out warranty*. If your child wears out his or her clothes while they still fit, Sears will give you new ones. And that sure beats sewing on patches.

"How can someone that light be that hard on clothes?"

3. *It lets your kids choose form over 70 big-name brands*. Levi's®. Oshkosh®. Bugle Boy®. Because the biggest waste of money of all is buying something your child won't wear.

"Was I that particular when I was a kid?"

4. *Low, sensible prices*. Growth spurts don't wait for sales. So we start with a good price every day.

"It's a growing race. Your kid vs. your budget."

B

Seabell boys' fleece sets. Fun, sporty, and practical, these 2-piece sets are great for your active guy. Choose the football or basketball style, both in sizes 8–14. Priced to really move, just $19.99, at Kmart.

EXAMPLE **12**

CONSUMER

Background. These full-page advertisements ran in the same October issue of *Ladies' Home Journal*. Ad A ran on page 119, and Ad B appeared on page 27. *Ladies' Home Journal* contains highly focused features and articles that address a variety of special interests, including beauty and fashion, food and nutrition, health and medicine, home decorating and design, parenting and self-help, personalities, and current events. Which of these advertisements do you think obtained higher Gallup & Robinson scores among women readers?

STUDENT ANALYSIS

NAME _____ CLASS _____ DATE _____

EXAMPLE 13

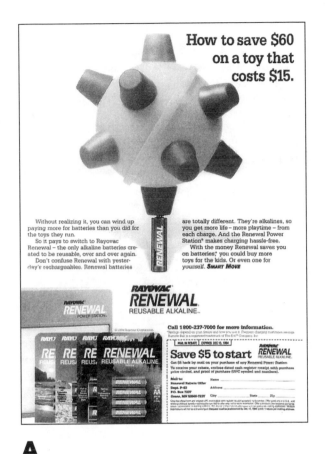

A

B

Without realizing it, you can wind up paying more for batteries than you did for the toys they run.

So it pays to switch to Rayovac Renewal—the only alkaline batteries created to be reusable, over and over again.

Don't confuse Renewal with yesterday's rechargeables. Renewal batteries are totally different. They're alkalines, so you get more life—more playtime—from each charge. And the renewal Power Station® makes charging hassle-free.

With the money Renewal saves you on batteries, you could buy more toys for the kids. Or even one for yourself. Smart move.

Nothing outlasts the Energizer. They keep going and going and going.

EXAMPLE **13**

CONSUMER

Background. As the name suggests, *People* magazine, in which Ad A appeared, has an absorbing interest in the lives and doings of people, including celebrities and ordinary people whose lives have taken different and interesting turns. Mostly, however, it is aimed at sophisticated men and women who are pacesetters. Much is made of the lifestyles and work of people in the arts, sciences, business, politics, entertainment, and sports. Ad A ran in full page size in October. Ad B, another full-page advertisement, ran four years earlier in *Time* magazine. This publication reports on national and international news, accompanied by much analysis and commentary. A variety of topics are presented, including lifestyles, the arts, health, business, the economy, the Washington scene, science, technology, personal business, and current affairs. Which of these advertisements do you think obtained higher Gallup & Robinson scores among men readers?

STUDENT ANALYSIS

NAME _____ CLASS _____ DATE _____

EXAMPLE 14

A

Concentrated Stain Maker.

Concentrated Stain Remover.

Remove tough stains—from grass to grease—with Shout® Concentrated Gel. The power of a gel. The penetration of a brush. Really tough stains have just met their match.

B

All the clean that sensitive skin needs.

New "all" free clear's dermatologist-tested formula has all the stain-fighting power of "all," so even if you have sensitive skin, you don't have to compromise on a bit of clean. It has the pure cleaning power of "all." But with no perfumes or dyes added to irritate your family's skin.

EXAMPLE 14

CONSUMER

Background.   Both of these full-page advertisements ran in women's magazines: Ad A in a September issue of *Ladies' Home Journal* and Ad B in a June issue of *Good Housekeeping* three years before. *Ladies' Home Journal* contains highly focused features and articles that reflect varied interests, such as beauty and fashion, food and nutrition, health and medicine, home decorating and design, parenting, and self-help. *Good Housekeeping* is aimed at the "New Traditionalist." Articles that focus on food, fitness, beauty, and child care draw upon the resources of the *Good Housekeeping* institute. Editorial material includes human interest stories, articles that focus on social issues, money management, health news, travel, and the "Better Way," an eight-page guide to better living. Which of these advertisements do you think obtained better Gallup & Robinson scores among women readers?

STUDENT ANALYSIS

NAME _____ CLASS _____ DATE _____

EXAMPLE **15**

A

Later, Mom. Achoo! Slap me five! A slippery five—yuck!

Gross!

Hack!

Slimed again!

Yeeeaauck!

I'm home!

. . . And into the tub!

Washing with Safeguard eliminates germs your family has picked up along the way.

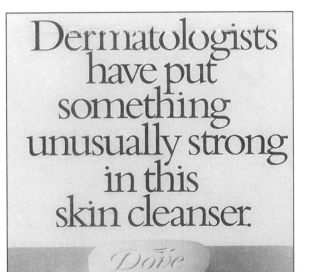

B

Eighty-two percent of dermatologists recommend Dove® in an average week. They know that it won't dry your face like soap. Because Dove isn't a soap. It cleans thoroughly, without disturbing the skin's outer layer the way soap can. And that's why dermatologists recommend Dove. And why you can trust Dove, with its 1/4 cleansing cream formula, to leave your skin feeling soft and smooth. Every time you wash.

EXAMPLE 15

CONSUMER

Background. *People* magazine carried Ad A in November. Ad B ran in *Ladies' Home Journal* in June of the same year. Both were full-page advertisements. *People* focuses on personalities in all fields, from the famous to the infamous and ordinary to unusual, and serves as a guide to personalities and events currently in the limelight in the arts, science, business, motion pictures, television, politics, books, records, and sports. *Ladies' Home Journal* addresses a variety of special interests, such as beauty and fashion, food and nutrition, parenting and self-help, health and medicine, home decorating and design, personalities, and current events. Which of these advertisements do you think obtained higher Gallup & Robinson scores among women readers?

STUDENT ANALYSIS

NAME _____ CLASS _____ DATE _____

EXAMPLE **16**

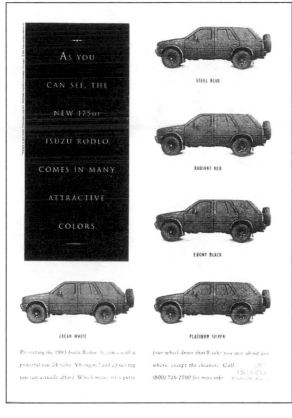

A

As you can see, the new 175hp Isuzu Rodeo comes in many attractive colors.

Presenting the 1993 Isuzu Rodeo. It comes with a powerful new 24-valve, V6 engine, and a price tag you can actually afford. Which means it's a gutsy four-wheel drive that'll take you just about anywhere, except the cleaners. Call (800) 726-2700 for more info.

B

The 5th unwritten law of driving. If there is a hole in the road you will hit it.

The new Isuzu Trooper has been thoughtfully redesigned around a rather jarringly obvious point: city infrastructures are falling apart. Which tends to make driving on the road feel a lot like driving off the road, which is why the new Trooper is equipped with an incredibly smooth, quiet suspension system that doesn't know the difference.

EXAMPLE 16

CONSUMER

Background. *Sports Illustrated*, the bible for those interested in the world of sports, carried both of these full-page advertisements. Ad A ran in June; Ad B ran in the same month in the preceding year. In addition to covering major games and events, *Sports Illustrated* offers colorful commentary on individuals in sports and on the place of sports in contemporary life. Articles also appear on fashion, physical fitness, and conservation. Which of these advertisements do you think obtained higher Gallup & Robinson scores among men readers?

STUDENT ANALYSIS

NAME _____ CLASS _____ DATE _____

EXAMPLE 17

A

Your mouth will say merci.

French Vanilla Cafe.

The taste of creamy, rich coffee. Kissed with the flavor of vanilla.

B

General Foods® International Coffees

New Italian Cappuccino

More than just a cup of coffee.

EXAMPLE 17

CONSUMER

Background. Ad A, a full-page advertisement, ran in *Cosmopolitan* in August. Ad B, also a full-page advertisement, ran in an April issue of *People* two years later. *Cosmopolitan* is edited for young women of today, dealing with the emotional side of their lives. Articles include such issues as relationships, careers, science, money, travel, fashion, beauty, food, and decorating. Also, there are celebrity profiles and fiction. *People* focuses on compelling personalities in all fields, from the known to the unknown, the famous to the infamous, the ordinary to the extraordinary; it serves as a guide to who and what are important in the arts, science, business, politics, television, motion pictures, books, records, and sports. Which of these advertisements do you think obtained higher Gallup & Robinson scores among women readers?

STUDENT ANALYSIS

NAME _____ CLASS _____ DATE _____

EXAMPLE **18**

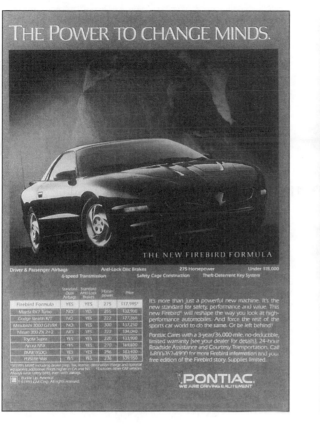

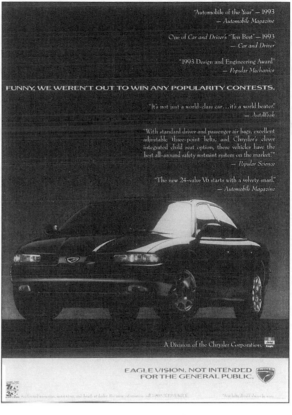

A

It's more than just a powerful new machine. It's the new standard for safety, performance, and value. This new Firebird® will reshape the way you look at high-performance automobiles. And force the rest of the sports car world to do the same. Or be left behind.

Pontiac Cares with a 3-year/36,000-mile, no-deductible, limited warranty (see your dealer for details), 24-hour Roadside Assistance and Courtesy Transportation. Call 1-800-762-4900 for more Firebird information and your free edition of the Firebird story. Supplies limited.

B

"Automobile of the Year"—1993
   —*Automobile Magazine*

One of *Car and Driver's* "Ten Best"—1993
   —*Car and Driver*

"1993 Design and Engineering Award"
   —*Popular Mechanics*

"It's not just a world-class car . . . it's a world beater."
   —*AutoWeek*

"With standard driver and passenger air bags, excellent adjustable three-point belts, and Chrysler's clever integrated child seat option, these vehicles have the best all-around safety restraint system on the market."
   —*Popular Science*

"The new 24-valve V6 starts with a velvety snarl."
   —*Automobile Magazine*

Funny, we weren't out to win any popularity contests.

EXAMPLE **18**

CONSUMER

Background. Both of these full-page advertisements ran in *Sports Illustrated*, Ad A in October and Ad B in February of the same year. *Sports Illustrated*'s beat is the world of sports, which it interprets and covers in depth. It covers major games and events and conveys the character and spirit of both. There is much comment on individuals in sports and the place of sports in contemporary life. Articles are included on fashion, physical fitness, and conservation. A popular yearly offering is the magazine's swimsuit issue. Which of these advertisements do you think obtained higher Gallup & Robinson scores among men readers?

STUDENT ANALYSIS

NAME _____ CLASS _____ DATE _____

EXAMPLE **19**

A

What's gotten into the Wainwrights?

Could be it's the Kretschmer® Wheat Germ they've been sprinkling on their foods. It's a good source of protein, essential vitamins, minerals, and fiber that adds a healthy zip to your diet. And quite possibly to your step, too.

B

Kretschmer Wheat Germ.

It can't promise to grow hair on your head. But it can top your favorite ice cream with natural vitamins, minerals, and fiber—plus a delicious, crunchy taste.

That's because Kretschmer is the heart of the wheat—the storehouse of concentrated nutrition.

So add Honey Crunch Kretschmer to your ice cream—or frozen yogurt—and see what its delicious crunch and great nutrition can do for you!

Kretschmer. It's the Heart of the Wheat.

EXAMPLE **19**

CONSUMER

Background. Ad A ran in *Better Homes and Gardens* in August, and Ad B appeared in *Bon Appétit* in June, four years earlier. Both were full-page advertisements. *Better Homes and Gardens* provides home service information for people who have a serious interest in their homes. It provides in-depth coverage of home and family subjects, including food and appliances, building and handyman, decorating, family money management, gardening, travel, health, automobiles, home and family entertainment, new product information, and shopping. *Bon Appétit* focuses on sophisticated home entertaining, with emphasis on food and its presentation. Also, there are features on fine tableware, kitchen design, travel, and restaurants. Regular departments cover tableware and products; food-related collectibles; health and nutrition; quick recipes for weekday meals; cooking techniques; wine and spirits; and recipes from restaurants, hotels, and inns around the world. Which of these advertisements do you think obtained higher Gallup & Robinson scores among women readers?

STUDENT ANALYSIS

NAME _____ CLASS _____ DATE _____

EXAMPLE 20

A

B

Beefier Beef.

Beef up the flavor with Kikkoman Soy Sauce. As the only major brand of soy sauce that's naturally brewed, Kikkoman has the unique ability to enhance, not overpower, the natural flavors of food. Beef becomes beefier. And any great taste you create becomes a bit tastier. Naturally. For some exceptional recipes using Kikkoman Sauces, send a stamped, self-addressed envelope to: Kikkoman International Inc., Dept. CSCD, P.O. Box 420784, San Francisco, CA 94142-0784.

Kikkoman. It's a matter of taste.

Tabasco® brings out the unexpected in food.

The lively taste of Tabasco® sauce. Don't keep it bottled up.

EXAMPLE 20

CONSUMER

Background. Ad A was advertised in the *Ladies' Home Journal* in February, and Ad B ran in *Life* in September, two years earlier. Each advertisement was a full page. *Ladies' Home Journal* contains highly focused features and articles that address a variety of special interests, including beauty and fashion, food and nutrition, health and medicine, home decorating and design, parenting and self-help, person- alities, and current events. *Life* shows the world through the power of pictures. It covers domestic and international news, business, the arts, lifestyle, and human interest sto- ries. Each issue includes news stories, feature articles, regu- lar departments, and photo essays. Which of these advertise- ments do you think obtained higher Gallup & Robinson scores among women readers?

STUDENT ANALYSIS

NAME _____ CLASS _____ DATE _____

82

EXAMPLE 21

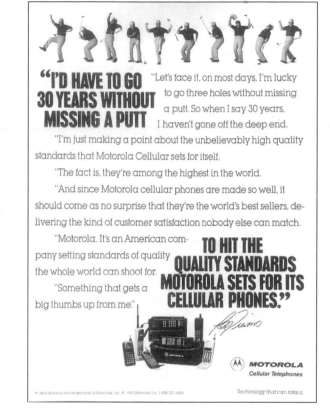

A

Sure, you can get better range this way, but why go to all the trouble? General Electric has developed a family of car phones that deliver extended-range performance and are a lot easier on your eyes and ears. The Carfone XR™ series.

We've combined the industry's hottest receiver with the FCC-maximum three watts of continuous power, making it one of the most important breakthroughs in cellular performance. You receive calls more distinctly and hold onto them longer.

Carfone XR™ includes 832 channels, which may make placing calls easier in larger cities. To make conversation safer, a hands-free speaker option is also available. And perhaps most importantly, it's backed by our limited three-year warranty.

The Carfone XR series™. We deliver the performance you want without making you look ridiculous in the process.

Test drive one today at leading cellular retailers. Or call 1-800-CARFONE.

B

"Let's face it, on most days, I'm lucky to go three holes without missing a putt. So when I say 30 years, I haven't gone off the deep end.

"I'm just making a point about the unbelievably high quality standards that Motorola Cellular sets for itself.

"The fact is, they're among the highest in the world.

"And since Motorola cellular phones are made so well, it should come as no surprise that they're the world's best sellers, delivering the kind of customer satisfaction nobody else can match.

"Motorola. It's an American company setting standards of quality the whole world can shoot for.

Something that gets a big thumbs up from me."

EXAMPLE 21

CONSUMER

Background. These one-page ads ran in *Business Week*; Ad A ran in September and Ad B appeared in November, four years later. *Business Week*, considered a high-level management publication, reports ideas and trends that can affect the economy or an industry. It also provides insights helpful to business executives in the operation of their own businesses. Some of the areas covered are finance, technology, media, marketing, government relations, science, information processing, labor, and social issues. Which of these advertisements do you think obtained higher Gallup & Robinson scores among male readers?

STUDENT ANALYSIS

NAME _____ CLASS _____ DATE _____

EXAMPLE 22

A

Colgate® Plus was designed by a team of scientists to accurately fit the shape of the human mouth. Its unique diamond-shaped head comfortably gets to difficult areas, like the back teeth. So it cleans throughly to help keep teeth strong and healthy. And that's the most comfortable feeling of all.

B

The Colgate® Plus Toothbrush has a unique design that works like a dental tool to fight bacterial plaque at home. The plus is its diamond-shaped head and dual bristles that help clean away plaque, even from between teeth.

So to cut plaque, get our diamond. The Colgate Plus Toothbrush. It's what you'd expect from Colgate, the world's leading toothbrush.

EXAMPLE 22

CONSUMER

Background. Ad A ran in *Ladies' Home Journal* in July, and Ad B appeared in *People* in June, two years before. *Ladies' Home Journal* addresses a variety of special interests, such as beauty and fashion, food and nutrition, parenting and self-help, health and medicine, home decorating and design, personalities, and current events. *People* focuses on personalities in all fields, from unknown to famous and ordinary to unusual, and serves as a guide to personalities and events currently in the limelight in the arts, science, business, motion pictures, television, politics, books, records, and sports. Which of these advertisements do you think obtained higher Gallup & Robinson scores among women readers?

STUDENT ANALYSIS

NAME _____ CLASS _____ DATE _____

EXAMPLE 23

A

Bake in Quaker Oatmeal goodness and watch them disappear!

B

Quaker Oats helps you add goodness to an all-time favorite goodie.

EXAMPLE 23

CONSUMER

Background. These full-page advertisements ran in *Ladies' Home Journal*; Ad A ran in November, and Ad B appeared in October, two years earlier. *Ladies' Home Journal* is edited with the informational needs of the modern woman in mind. Highly focused features and articles address a variety of special interests, including beauty and fashion, food and nutrition, health and medicine, home decorating and design, parenting and self-help, personalities, and current events. Which of these advertisements do you think obtained higher Gallup & Robinson scores among women readers?

STUDENT ANALYSIS

NAME _____ CLASS _____ DATE _____

EXAMPLE 24

A

Water, water everywhere. The slippery kind. That's when you'll sure be glad you've got Goodyear's all-season Aquatred®. Because Aquatred has an advanced deep-groove AquaChannel™ that sweeps water away at more than a gallon a second. Leaving you feeling secure and in control of the situation. So gear up for inclement weather. With AquaTred. Only from Goodyear.

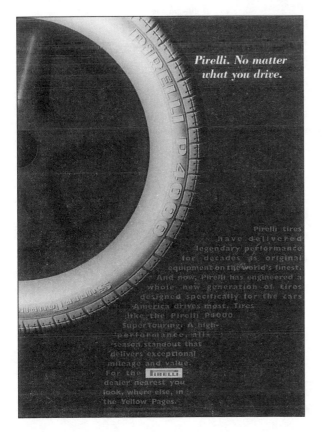

B

Pirelli tires have delivered legendary performance for decades as original equipment on the world's finest. And now, Pirelli has engineered a whole new generation of tires designed specifically for the cars America drives most. Tires like the Pirelli P4000 Super-Touring®. A high-performance, all-season standout that delivers exceptional mileage and value. For the Pirelli dealer nearest you look, where else, in the Yellow Pages.

EXAMPLE 24

CONSUMER

Background. These full-page ads ran in news magazines, with Ad A appearing in *Newsweek* in November, and Ad B running in *Time* magazine in April of the same year. *Newsweek* provides much commentary and analysis, along with reporting of weekly developments of world and national news. It presents trends in the economy, politics, the Washington scene, lifestyles, health, science, the arts, and technology. *Time*, too, reports news of national and world affairs, business, and lifestyles, with considerable use of photography, maps, and charts. Which of these advertisements do you think obtained higher Gallup & Robinson scores among men readers?

STUDENT ANALYSIS

NAME _____ CLASS _____ DATE _____

EXAMPLE 25

A

There's a name for decaffeinated tea that doesn't get lost in ice.

Lipton.

Every drop reflects the one-of-a-kind refreshment of Lipton® De caffeinated Tea. The one and only Lipton Tea taste that can stand tall in a glass of ice on a hot summer day. Decaffeinated naturally with pure, sparkling water and effervescence. The only thing that's lost is your thirst.

B

It's gone. It was so good. That crisp, clear taste. The flavor comes from those tiny tea leaves. That's definitely Tetley®. And it's why so many folks are switching to Tetley tea. Fill it up. Drink it down. Fill it up. Drink it down.

Betcha gonna like it better, too.™

EXAMPLE **25**

CONSUMER

Background. These full-page advertisements ran in *Better Homes and Gardens*; Ad A appeared in July, and Ad B ran in August of the following year. This publication provides information for people who have a serious interest in their homes. It provides in-depth coverage of home and family subjects, including food and appliances, building and handyman, decorating, family money management, gardening, travel, health, automobiles, home and family entertainment, new product information, and shopping. Which of these advertisements do you think obtained higher Gallup & Robinson scores among women readers?

STUDENT ANALYSIS

NAME _____ CLASS _____ DATE _____

EXAMPLE **26**

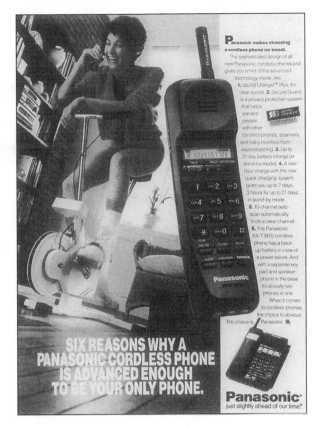

A

Don't be bound by convention.

The Sony Cordless telephone. . .

. . . technology that sets you free with an elegance of design that expresses your individuality.

B

Panasonic makes choosing a cordless phone no sweat.

The sophisticated design of all new Panasonic cordless phones just gives you a hint of the advanced technology inside, like:

1. Sound Charger™ Plus, for clear sound.
2. Secure Guard is a privacy protection system that helps prevent people with other cordless phones, scanners, and baby monitors from eavesdropping.
3. Up to 21-day battery charge (in stand-by mode).
4. A one-hour charge with the new quick charging system gives you up to 7 days, 3 hours for up to 21 days, in stand-by mode.
5. 10-channel auto-scan automatically finds a clear channel.
6. The Panasonic KX-T3970 cordless phone has a back-up battery in case of a power failure. And with a separate key pad and speaker-phone in the base it's actually two phones in one.

When it comes to cordless phones, the choice is obvious. The choice is Panasonic.

EXAMPLE **26**

CONSUMER

Background. Ad A ran in January issue of *Bon Appétit*, and Ad B ran in *Glamour* in December of the following year. Both advertisements were full pages. *Bon Appétit* focuses on sophisticated home entertainment, with emphasis on food and its preparation. Also included are features on fine tableware, kitchen design, travel, restaurants, health and nutrition, quick recipes, cooking techniques, wine and spirits, and recipes from around the world. *Glamour* is edited for the contemporary American woman. It informs her of the trends, recommends how she can adapt them to her needs, and motivates her to take action. More than half of *Glamour*'s editorial content focuses on fashion, beauty and health, and the coverage of personal relationships, travel, career, food, and entertainment. Which of these advertisements do you think obtained higher Gallup & Robinson scores among women readers?

STUDENT ANALYSIS

NAME _____ CLASS _____ DATE _____

EXAMPLE 27

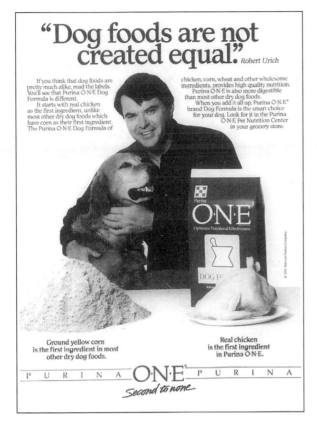

A

If you think that dog foods are pretty much alike, read the labels. You'll see that Purina O.N.E. Dog Formula is different.

It starts with real chicken as the first ingredient, unlike most other dry dog foods which have corn as their first ingredient. The Purina O.N.E. Dog Formula of chicken, corn, wheat, and other wholesome ingredients, provides high quality nutrition.

Purina O.N.E. is also more digestible than most other dry dog foods.

When you add it all up, Purina O.N.E.® Brand Dog Formula is the smart choice for your dog. Look for it in the Purina O.N.E. Pet Nutrition Center in your grocery store.

Ground yellow corn is the first ingredient in most other dry dog foods.

Real chicken is the first ingredient in Purina O.N.E.

B

Call 1-800-367-1226 for a free can of Reward.

With our offer for a free can of Reward, there's never been a better time to put its great taste to the test. Who knows? Your dog may even like Reward more than Mighty Dog brand dog food. So give us a call for a free can of Reward (unless, of course, your dog already has).

Reward. The taste lives up to the name.

EXAMPLE 27

CONSUMER

Background. These full-page advertisements ran in *People*; Ad A ran in February, and Ad B appeared in June of the same year. *People* is aimed at active, sophisticated men and women and provides an overview of the pacesetters in America. Emphasis is on the work and lifestyles of people in the arts, science, business, politics, entertainment, and sports. Which of these advertisements do you think obtained higher Gallup & Robinson scores among women readers?

STUDENT ANALYSIS

NAME _____ CLASS _____ DATE _____

EXAMPLE **28**

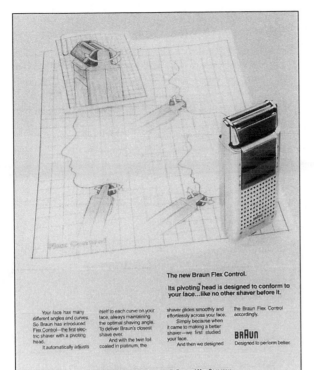

The new Braun Flex Control.

Its pivoting head is designed to conform to
your face...like no other shaver before it.

Your face has many
different angles and curves.
So Braun has introduced
Flex Control—the first electric shaver with a pivoting
head.
It automatically adjusts

itself to each curve on your
face, always maintaining
the optimal shaving angle.
To deliver Braun's closest
shave ever.
And with the twin foil
coated in platinum, the

shaver glides smoothly and
effortlessly across your face.
Simply because when
it came to making a better
shaver—we first studied
your face.
And then we designed

the Braun Flex Control
accordingly.

BRAUN
Designed to perform better.

Available at Hecht's, Kaufmann's, G. Fox, and May Company.

A

Your face has many different angles and curves. So Braun has introduced Flex Control—the first electronic shaver with a pivoting
head.

It automatically adjusts itself to every curve on your face, always
maintaining the optimal shaving angle. To deliver Braun's closest
shave ever.

And with the twin foil coated in platinum, the shaver glides
smoothly and effortlessly across your face.

Simply because when it came to making a better shaver—we first
studied your face.

And then we designed the Braun Flex Control accordingly.

TO FULLY APPRECIATE NORELCO'S INCREDIBLY CLOSE, COMFORTABLE SHAVE, YOU HAVE TO LOOK BENEATH THE SURFACE.

It's amazing, but true.
Norelco can actu-
ally shave *below* skin
level. And equally
amazing, Norelco can
shave you without
the blades even touch-
ing your skin.

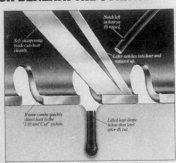

This feat is accom-
plished with a patented
technology unique
in all of shaving. The
"Lift and Cut" system.
Here, a precision

mechanism has been
engineered by posi-
tioning a lifter in front
of the blade. When
the lifter notches into
a hair, it lifts it up. As the
blade cuts it, the hair
shaft can actually drop
back *below* the skin.
The result is an in-
credibly close shave.
And because you can
shave without the
blades even touching
your face, it's incredibly
comfortable.

Try the Norelco.
And experience the
deep satisfaction of
a perfect shave.

Norelco
We make close comfortable.

B

It's amazing but true.

Norelco® can actually shave *below* skin level. And equally amazing, Norelco can shave you without the blades even touching your
skin.

This feat is accomplished with a patented technology unique in all
of shaving. The "Lift and Cut"™ system.

Here, a precision mechanism has been engineered by positioning
a lifter in front of the blade. When the lifter notches into a hair, it lifts
it up. As the blade cuts it, the hair shaft can actually drop back *below* the skin.

The result is an incredibly close shave. And because you can
shave without the blades even touching your face, it's incredibly
comfortable.

Try the Norelco. And experience the deep satisfaction of a perfect
shave.

EXAMPLE **28**

CONSUMER

Background. These full-page advertisements appeared in *U.S. News & World Report*. Ad A ran in June, and Ad B also ran in June of the same year, but Ad A was placed on page 27, and Ad B appeared on page 2. *U.S. News & World Report* covers international events and information on life management. It stresses new implications and trends rather than the events themselves. Each issue contains a section that highlights innovations in finance, technology, education, health care, and other matters of personal impact. Considering the relative page placements of these two advertisements, which do you think obtained higher Gallup & Robinson scores among men readers?

STUDENT ANALYSIS

NAME _____ CLASS _____ DATE _____

EXAMPLE 29

A

A delicious blend of sweet honey and tangy Dijon mustard. Without fat or cholesterol. One taste and you'll know what the buzz is all about.

If It Tastes Too Good To be Fat Free, It's Kraft Free.™

B

A recent taste test proved that among those with a preference, KRAFT® DELICIOUSLY LIGHT™ tasted better than WISH-BONE® full fat Italian dressing. So, with 1/3 less fat and all the taste you want, why not try KRAFT® DELICIOUSLY LIGHT™ yourself? After all, it's already been put to the test.

1/3 Less Fat With All The Taste You Want.

EXAMPLE 29

CONSUMER

Background. *Ladies' Home Journal* carried Ad A in July, and Ad B ran in *People* in June of the same year. Both advertisements were full pages. *Ladies' Home Journal* contains highly focused features and articles that address a variety of special interests, including beauty and fashion, food and nutrition, health and medicine, home decorating and design, parenting and self-help, personalities, and current events. *People* is aimed at active, sophisticated men and women and provides an overview of the pacesetters of America. Emphasis is on the work and lifestyles of people in the arts, science, business, politics, entertainment, and sports. Which of these advertisements do you think obtained higher Gallup & Robinson scores among women readers?

STUDENT ANALYSIS

NAME _____ CLASS _____ DATE _____

EXAMPLE 30

A

Introducing the new KitchenAid® Create-a-Cooktop System. The ingredients: electric grill, two-burner sealed gas unit, electric unit with two cast-iron elements, glass ceramic radiant/halogen unit, downdraft vent. In your choice of black, white or almond.

Mix or match the units to create a cooktop that matches the way you cook. Create one big cooktop. Or create two separate cooking stations. Create a separate warming station. Or create a separate grilling area. Use the sleek downdraft vent or an overhead exhaust system.

No matter how you design it, you'll get the same premium quality that has made KitchenAid dishwashers legendary.

To start creating your cooktop, just call the KitchenAid Consumer Assistance Center, 1-800-422-1230, for information and the name of the dealer nearest you.

B

Introducing the Expressions™ cooktop by Jenn-Air. The cooktop that lets you custom-design your own cooking surface. Select a finish from black or white tempered glass or professional-looking stainless steel. Then choose from 2, 4, or 6 burner sizes plus a variety of interchangeable cooking cartridges, control panels and optional plug-in accessories. Every Expressions cooktop comes with Jenn-Air's indoor grilling with downdraft ventilation. The grill grates have a non-stick Excalibur® coating that wipes clean easily. And almost all of the pieces can be cleaned in the dishwasher. See the new Expressions cooktop at your Jenn-Air dealer. It's truly revolutionary.

EXAMPLE **30**

CONSUMER

Background. Both of these advertisements were full pages. Ad A ran in a June issue of *Better Homes and Gardens*, while Ad B appeared in *Bon Appétit* in January of the same year. *Better Homes and Gardens* offers information to people who have a serious interest in their homes. It covers food and appliances, building and handyman, decorating, family money management, gardening, travel, health, automobiles, home and family entertainment, new product information, and current events. *Bon Appétit* focuses on sophisticated home entertaining, emphasizing food and its presentation. Regular departments include new tableware and products; food related collectibles; health and nutrition; quick recipes for weekday meals; entertaining; cooking techniques; wine and spirits; and recipes from restaurants, hotels, and inns around the world. Which of these advertisements do you think obtained higher Gallup & Robinson scores among women readers?

STUDENT ANALYSIS

NAME _____ CLASS _____ DATE _____

EXAMPLE 31

A

B

It's not just about exercise anymore, is it?

It's not about inches. It's not about "working off" your meals. It's definitely not about what's "in." It's not even about fitness. It's about goals, and personal bests, and training.

That's why it's about time you got into a serious training shoe like the ASICS® GEL-120. Technically speaking, it's loaded: Gel shock absorption in the rearfoot, a blown rubber outsole with AHAR heel plug for durability, and for the first time in any ASICS GEL shoe, width sizing.

Historically speaking, the GEL-120 is the latest and best extension of our highly acclaimed GEL-100 series. Just plain speaking, *Runner's World* magazine says it's hard to find a better shoe for the price.

But when all is said and done, it comes down to one thing: performance. And ASICS has been a running performance leader for 20 years. So drive on down and get a shoe to fit your goals: the GEL-120. Better yet, run. After all, a little exercise never hurt anyone.

The Air Huarache™ from Nike. The shoe that stretches with your foot.

EXAMPLE 31

CONSUMER

Background. Both of these full-page advertisements ran in the same issue of *Sports Illustrated*, with Ad A appearing on page 63 and Ad B running on page 9. *Sports Illustrated* is concerned with the world of sports, recreation, and active leisure. Major games and events are previewed, analyzed, and commented on. Much attention is given to individuals in sports. Often the magazine goes beyond mere reporting of sports to evaluate the part sports play in contemporary life. Attention is also paid to such matters as physical fitness, conservation, and fashion. There are special departments that concern sports equipment, statistics, and books. Which of these advertisements do you think obtained higher Gallup & Robinson scores among men readers?

STUDENT ANALYSIS

NAME _____ CLASS _____ DATE _____

EXAMPLE **32**

A

Make it in honor of Uncle Sam. Uncle Steve. Aunt Nina. Their Kids . . .

B

What's in it for you.

70% skim milk. A big hug. Wholesome snack. Crowd control after school. Fresh from the dairy case. Cool mom status. One for yourself (if you're fast).

What's in it for kids.

Awesome taste. Awesome chocolate. Awesome vanilla. Totally awesome.

Jell-O Pudding Snacks. Something in 'em for everyone.

EXAMPLE **32**

CONSUMER

Background. Ad A ran in the *Ladies' Home Journal* in July; Ad B appeared in *Better Homes and Gardens* in March of the preceding year. Both advertisements were full pages. *Ladies' Home Journal* contains highly focused features and articles that address a variety of special interests, including beauty and fashion, food and nutrition, health and medicine, home decorating and design, parenting and self-help, personalities, and current events. *Better Homes and Gardens* provides home service information for people who have a serious interest in their homes. It provides in-depth coverage of home and family subjects, including food and appliances, building and handyman, decorating, family money management, gardening, travel, health, automobiles, entertainment, new product information, and shopping. Which of these advertisements do you think obtained higher Gallup & Robinson scores among women readers?

STUDENT ANALYSIS

NAME _____ CLASS _____ DATE _____

EXAMPLE **33**

A

Panasonic introduces the Palmcorder™. It's VHS! So its tapes will play in your VHS recorder.

Be careful, or you could end up with a compact camcorder that shoots tapes that can't play in your VHS recorder. Instead they force you to connect your camcorder to your TV every time you want to watch your tapes.

Not with the new Panasonic PV-41 Palmcorder camcorder. It's VHS. There are no loose wires or complicated connections. Its tapes simply slip into the included PlayPak which slides into any VHS recorder just like ordinary tape.

This Palmcorder has Digital Electronic Image Stabilization. It can help hold the picture steady when your hand shakes. Plus, there's a 12 to 1 digital zoom, 4 lux low-light capability and a 5 watt color enhancement light.

So before you buy a compact camcorder, Panasonic has a good question for you . . . "Will its tapes play in your VCR?"

B

Whether it's summer vacation, a winter excursion, or just hanging around, capture it all on America's most popular camcorder. The Sony Handycam®. It's more than just hi-fi stereo, two hours of recording time, and Sony's bright, sharp 8mm picture. It's the easiest and most creative way to document your life.

EXAMPLE **33**

CONSUMER

Background. Ad A ran in an October issue of *People* magazine, a publication that is aimed at active, sophisticated men and women and provides an overview of the pacesetters in America. Emphasis is on the work and lifestyles of people in the arts, science, business, politics, entertainment, and sports. *U.S. News* carried Ad B in a November issue of the same year. This magazine covers world events, with information on life management. It focuses on news implications and trends rather than on the events themselves. One section reports innovations in technology, finance, health care, education, and other matters. Both ads are full page. Which of these advertisements do you think obtained higher Gallup & Robinson scores among men readers?

STUDENT ANALYSIS

NAME _____ CLASS _____ DATE _____

EXAMPLE **34**

A

You can't plan those big moments. But with the right camcorder, you can be ready to capture them when they happen.

Take the new Canon UC1, for instance. It's so slim and small you can take it anywhere. And yet, it's packed with many of the top features of our best 8mm models. Advances like precision optics and the wireless remote control found in our affordable E65 and sophisticated L1 Canonvision 8 camcorders.

So why let your big moments get away, when Canon can give you so many ways to catch them.

B

Panasonic Palmcorder™ Camcorder tapes play in the VHS VCR. Not all camcorder brands can do that.

Which camcorder would you buy? One of those whose tapes play in your VCR? Or one whose tapes don't? This isn't a trick question. There are actually some camcorders that shoot tapes that can't play in your VHS VCR.

But the Panasonic Palmcorder Camcorders are VHS. Their tapes can play in your VCR. Your family's, your friends', any one of 70 million VHS recorders out there. All you need is its included Play-Pak. There are no wires to connect. The other kind of camcorder must be connected to your TV. And since you need the camcorder to both shoot and play back, it gets twice the wear.

Sharing tapes from those other camcorders can be a real problem. Because practically everyone has a VHS recorder, you have to find a way of converting those tapes to VHS. Why not start out with a VHS camcorder to begin with? No matter how you look at it, the choice is obvious. The new Panasonic Palmcorder Camcorder.

EXAMPLE 34

CONSUMER

Background. These full-page advertisements ran in *People*; Ad A appeared in a December issue, and Ad B ran in November, two years later. *People* focuses on compelling personalities of our time, from the known to the unknown, the famous to the infamous, and the ordinary to the extraordinary. The publication is a guide to the persons and events that are currently in the public eye in the arts, science, business, politics, television, movies, books, records, and sports. Which of these advertisements do you think obtained higher Gallup & Robinson scores among women readers?

STUDENT ANALYSIS

NAME _____ CLASS _____ DATE _____

EXAMPLE 35

A

Nothing warms 'em like hot oatmeal (except maybe a hug).

Instant Quaker® Oatmeal. It's The Right Thing To Do.

B

For moms who have a lot of love, but not a lot of time.

Guess what! In 90 seconds flat—about the same time it takes to make cold cereal—you can make Instant Quaker® Oatmeal. She'll get piping-hot Quaker Oats nutrition—in flavors she loves. And you'll both get a nice, warm feeling inside!

EXAMPLE 35

CONSUMER

Background. Ad A ran in *Good Housekeeping* in January; Ad B ran in *People* in October of the same year. Both advertisements were full pages. *Good Housekeeping* is edited for the "New traditionalist." Articles focusing on food, fitness, beauty, and child care draw upon the resources of the *Good Housekeeping* institute. Editorial includes human interest stories, articles that focus on social issues, money management, health news, and travel. *People*, aimed at active, sophisticated men and women, provides an overview of the pacesetters in America. Emphasis is on the work and lifestyles of people in the arts, science, business, politics, entertainment, and sports. Which of these advertisements do you think obtained higher Gallup & Robinson scores among women readers?

STUDENT ANALYSIS

NAME _____ CLASS _____ DATE _____

EXAMPLE **36**

A

Remember when Japanese cars meant high quality at reasonable prices? Apparently the Japanese don't. The average price of a Japanese car is approaching what the average American family makes in a year. The good news is that one company still builds the kind of cars for which Japan was renowned.

Our cars are made with pride in Korea. At some of the industry's most sophisticated plants, we turn out quality cars filled with advanced engineering and safety features and back them with outstanding customer care. And thanks to Korea's dollar-friendly economy they're still affordable. See that stylish sedan in the picture? It's our 1994 Elantra. It has a driver's side airbag, offers one of the world's most advanced anti-lock braking systems and comes with features you'd expect in a luxury car. Yet it starts at less than $10,000.

Why not call 1-800-826-CARS and ask one of our Hyundai Motor America family why an Elantra test drive makes sense for yours. We're conveniently located 6,587 miles east and thousands of dollars south of Japan.

B

Far be it from us to say you can't have whatever your heart desires. And at a price you can afford. So, right now, your Nissan® Dealer is leasing three of the most exciting cars you can drive. The legendary 300ZX®, the sports car of sports cars; the super handling, rear-wheel drive 240SX®; and the car that defines fun, the T-top NX™ 1600. Each with sports car driving technology. Each yours with no down payment on a 36-month lease.

Of course, this kind of lease program doesn't come along very often. So visit your Nissan Dealer soon. All you've got to say is, ''I want it.''

EXAMPLE **36**

CONSUMER

Background. Ad A appeared in *Time* magazine in a December issue. Ad B ran in *Newsweek* in June of the preceding year. Both magazines cover national and world news, and both offer much interpretation of that news. Each has a number of departments. *Time*, for example, covers lifestyles, entertainment, business, and photography. *Newsweek* offers coverage of politics, the economy, the Washington scene, the arts, health, science, and technology. Each advertisement was a full page. Which of these advertisements do you think obtained higher Gallup & Robinson scores among men readers?

STUDENT ANALYSIS

NAME _____ CLASS _____ DATE _____

EXAMPLE 37

A

When guests arrive from across town or from across the country, reward their night's stay with a restful sleep on a La-Z-Boy sleep sofa. Its innerspring mattress with extra length gives it bed-like comfort. And that makes it every bit as wonderful to sleep on as it is to look at. For a free brochure and the name of your nearest La-Z-Boy dealer, call 1-800-THEN RELAX (1-800-843-6735).

B

EXAMPLE 37

CONSUMER

Background. Ad A ran in *People* in March, and Ad B appeared in *Metropolitan Home* in June of the preceding year. Both Ad A and Ad B were full-page advertisements. *People*, a magazine aimed at active, sophisticated men and women, provides an overview of the pacesetters in America. Emphasis is on the work and lifestyles of people in the arts, science, business, politics, entertainment, and sports.

Metropolitan Home contains coverage of home design, home furnishings, fashion, food, wines and spirits, entertaining, electronics, and travel, with an editorial focus on the art of living well. It is edited for quality-conscious young adults and contains news and guidance toward achieving personal style. Which of these advertisements do you think obtained higher Gallup & Robinson scores among women readers?

STUDENT ANALYSIS

NAME _____ CLASS _____ DATE _____

EXAMPLE **38**

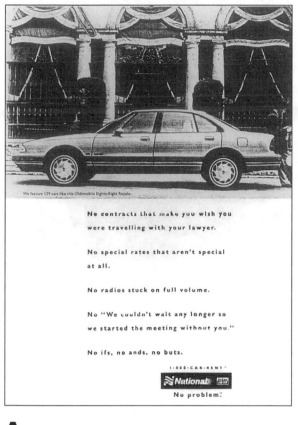

A

No contracts that make you wish you were travelling with your lawyer.

No special rates that aren't special at all.

No radios stuck on full volume.

No ''we couldn't wait any longer so we started the meeting without you.''

No ifs, no ands, and no buts.

B

When you're a member of Hertz #1 Club Gold®, there's no stopping at counters, no paperwork, nothing to slow you down. At 28 major airports, ''Gold'' is the fastest, easiest way ever to rent. It's another way #1 has more going for you.

EXAMPLE **38**

CONSUMER

Background. *Time* magazine and *Forbes* are logical choices for car rental advertising, because both have high readership among business travelers, the primary target of the rental companies. Ad A and Ad B are full-page advertisements. Ad A appeared in an August issue of *Time*. *Time* reports news of national and world affairs, as well as reporting and commenting on business, politics, and the economy. Politics and the Washington scene are covered in depth.

Ad B ran in a December issue of *Forbes*, a year and a half before Ad A. *Forbes* is a high-level business magazine aimed at top management and those who aspire to the executive suites. Many topics are covered, including global trends, taxes, computers, marketing, law, communications, and technology for business managers. Which of these advertisements do you think obtained higher Gallup & Robinson scores among male readers?

STUDENT ANALYSIS

NAME _____ CLASS _____ DATE _____

EXAMPLE **39**

A

It's time to stop wishing you were Eric Burdon. The Pioneer LaserKaraoke® CLD-V820 Combination CD/LaserDisc™ Player lets you sing lead on classics like *We Gotta Get Out of This Place*. And then backs you up with the instrumentals, a music video, and on-screen lyrics.

The CLD-V820 comes with Digital Signal Processing to make your living room sound like a Hall, a Stage, or an Arena. And it plays a constantly-growing library of over 1,000 hits, including your favorites from the '50s through the '90s.

After you've sung your heart out, relax with your favorite CDS or LaserDisc movies. With digital sound and a 60% sharper picture than standard VHS, the CLD-V820 is an ideal home theater component. It even plays both sides of LaserDisc movies automatically.

For more information or for the dealer nearest you, call (800) 421-1404 and ask for LaserKaraoke. And get ready to launch the next British invasion from the comfort of your own living room.

B

Panasonic Multi Laser Disc Players. They can play CDs and movies that look and sound incredible.

Imagine a CD player that also plays the thousands of movies and videos available on laser discs. That's the programmable LX101, a multi laser disc player that plays all five types of discs.

It has digital Y/C and digital time base correction for uncompromising video quality. Along with a scan function and shuttle that lets you see a clear picture in forward or reverse.

And for equally sharp sound, its MASH digital audio technology reproduces even the faintest sound to its fullest.

So when there's a multi laser disc player that looks and sounds this sensational, why settle for anything less?

To speak to a Panasonic dealer nearest you about our Multi Laser Disc Players, call 1-800-365-1515, ext. 456.

EXAMPLE **39**

CONSUMER

Background. Both of these full-page advertisements ran in *Playboy* magazine, a general interest, lifestyle publication for men. Ad A appeared in January; Ad B ran in January of the preceding year. *Playboy* zeroes in on the varied interest of men, such as motion pictures, sports, cars, fashion, and sophisticated entertaining. Profiles of politicians, athletes, and entertainers are featured. Much attention is given to editorial material and advertising that describe items that make up the "good life," such as the latest in electronic equipment. Which of these advertisements do you think obtained higher Gallup & Robinson scores among men readers?

STUDENT ANALYSIS

NAME _____ CLASS _____ DATE _____

EXAMPLE **40**

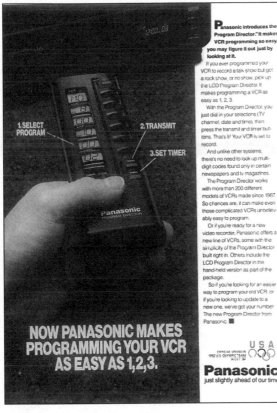

A

Panasonic introduces the Program Director™. It makes VCR programming so easy, you may figure it out just by looking at it.

If you ever programmed your VCR to record a talk show, but got a rock show, or no show, pick up the LCD Program Director. It makes programming a VCR as easy as 1, 2, 3.

With the Program Director, you just dial in your selections (TV channel, date and time), then press the transmit and timer buttons. That's it! Your VCR is set to record.

And unlike other systems, there's no need to look up multi-digit codes found only in certain newspapers and tv magazines.

The Program Director works with more than 200 models of VCRs made since 1987. So chances are, it can make even those complicated VCRs unbelievably easy to program.

Of, if you're ready for a new video recorder, Panasonic offers a new line of VCRs, some with the Program Director built right in. Others include the LCD Program Director in the handheld version as part of the package.

So if you're looking for an easier way to program your old VCR, or if you're looking to update a new one, we've got your number. The new Program Director from Panasonic.

B

Before attempting the operation of the Lifestyle® 12 home theater system, the following instructions should be carefully reviewed and memorized. *Push.*

[". . .operation is very intuitive . . . It offers style, versatility, and big sound in a small package."—Home Theater Technology]

One button. That's all it takes to experience the dramatic sound of the Bose® Lifestyle® 12 home theater system.

This is the surround sound system that simplifies home theater. Instead of a tower of components, you get a music center with CD player/tuner built in. Five acoustically matched speakers, each small enough to hold in the palm of your hand. And an easily hidden Acoustimass® bass module. (Not shown, because you won't see it in your home, either.) However, there is one last instruction you should follow. Hold onto your seat—after all, the sound is from Bose.

For more information and names of retailers near you, just push these buttons: 1-800-444-BOSE ext. 478.

EXAMPLE 40

CONSUMER

Background. Both of these full-page advertisements ran in *People* magazine; Ad A appeared in October, and Ad B ran in December, two years later. *People* focuses on compelling personalities of our time, from the known to the unknown, the famous to the infamous, and the ordinary to the extraordinary. *People* is a guide to important people and events in the arts, science, business, politics, television, movies, books, records, and sports. Which of these advertisements do you think obtained higher Gallup & Robinson scores among women readers?

STUDENT ANALYSIS

NAME _____ CLASS _____ DATE _____

The following 10 sets of Business Advertisements were tested by Readex, Inc.

EXAMPLE **41**

A

We can save weight on all kinds of components. No big secret. Aluminum weighs less than steel and that can mean the weight savings that you need to meet CAFE regulations.

We can save engineering costs. Something new. We have extensive experience in developing design and technology for light metals manufacturing (like the innovative "teacup" design indicated) and we're ready to share it in off-the-shelf packages. That will lower your development investment and reduce the premium usually associated with using aluminum alloys.

We can help you sell more cars. For the future. As of today, 75 percent of your customers are willing to spend more for environmentally responsible products. That number will increase by the time the car on which you're working hits the show room floor and aluminum offers recognized recyclability, proven fuel efficiency and superior corrosion resistance without E-coating.

We want to talk with you. About bumpers, lids, panels, trim, components and sub-assemblies. A free cost/weight analysis for your project is available from R.C. Pascasio, Alcoa Technical Center, New Kensington, PA. or call 1/800/237/3254.

See us at SAE '90, in booth 2456.

B

Optimization of design and material. Using Alcoa Automotive Systems allows you to tap into extensive technological resources, including FEM testing developed especially for aluminum alloys. Our off-the-shelf technologies, like the innovative teacup design for deck lids illustrated, will help you speed your design process. We can help you optimize component design and alloy selection to match or exceed your performance requirements.

Utilization of your existing resources. Aluminum substitution usually means you keep the same capital investment machinery, tooling and machine operators. A selection of over 90 TIC produced alloys and our experience in tool design, forming, and joining will complement your manufacturing capabilities.

Lightweighting at a lighter cost. Reducing upfront design time. Maintaining current setup and production cycle time. Minimizing scrap, and recycling (at a cost return), what scrap there is. These are the things that minimize the premium that sometimes can be associated with using aluminum alloys.

These services and technologies are applicable to panels, lids, bumpers, jacks, door beams, seats, and many other components. A free cost/weight analysis for your project is available from our staff of sales/application engineers. Direct inquiries to Alcoa Automotive Systems, 4000 Town Center, Suite 1370, Southfield, MI 48075 or call 313-352-4810.

EXAMPLE 41

BUSINESS

Background. These full-page, color advertisements ran for Alcoa in *Ward's Auto World*, a monthly publication. Readership for this magazine is composed of engineers and designers and people in manufacturing, production, sales, marketing, and communications in the automobile industry.

Subject matter includes market trends, extravehicular activities, manufacturing and materials, labor lookout, technology, and trends. Which advertisement do you think was scored higher by Readex?

STUDENT ANALYSIS

NAME _____ CLASS _____ DATE _____

EXAMPLE 42

A

Educators at all levels are making quite a significant discovery in classrooms across America. This discovery is supported by ongoing scientific research indicating a direct correlation between eating properly—beginning with a nutritious breakfast—and performing successfully all day long.

Healthy students are inquisitive and eager to learn. Those who begin the day with products carrying the ProPlus® signature receive long lasting protein nutrition—the kind needed to build strong bodies and attentive minds. And products with ProPlus Brand Isolated Soy Protein help school food service professionals meet the Dietary Guidelines for fat and sodium. That's good news all around, because children learn in school that healthy eating habits have life-long benefits.

Another pleasant discovery students are making about products with the ProPlus la-

bel is that "good for you" food can taste good, too. School food service professionals serving menu favorites such as pizza, hot dogs, chicken nuggets, fish sandwiches, tacos, breakfast biscuit sandwiches, teach students to make healthy choices from a variety of foods that are lower in fat, cholesterol, and sodium.

The lesson is clear. Education and good nutrition go hand in hand. Students who start each morning with products that bear the trusted signature of ProPlus have a good start on performing at their physical and mental best.

To receive a free information packet on how products with the ProPlus signature can help encourage good performance, call 1-800-325-7108.

B

Jimmy isn't a fussy eater. He simply likes all-beef taste in his burgers. No "funny" stuff. The only problem is that all-beef patties cost a bundle.

Luckily, some companies offer you a solution—a way to serve all-beef taste without paying an all-beef price.

The solution is ProPlus® isolated soy protein, the high-quality protein that performs like lean-beef protein.

ProPlus delivers good taste students like. Unlike soy concentrates or soy flours, ProPlus is bland tasting. So, even at the maximum 30% replacement level for pre-cooked patties, ProPlus won't make your students wonder what you put in their burgers. And ProPlus won't require extra seasoning to mask any "funny" taste.

In a scientifically controlled study involving 1,000 school children, students liked beef/

isolated soy protein patties just as much as they liked all-beef patties.

But taste isn't everything. ProPlus is over 90% pure protein, with no cholesterol and virtually no fat. So patties made with ProPlus make good nutritional sense, too. What's more, they cook up moist and succulent, and they stay that way on the serving line.

Products that carry the ProPlus signature provide you with an economical way to do a lot of good at once. They keep your students happy and reduce plate waste. And they help maintain high nutritional standards by assuring reduced fat, cholesterol and sodium. In short, products that say ProPlus supply you with better value.

For the names of companies who offer products made with ProPlus or to request our free ProPlus information packet, call 1-800/344-6937 or write: ProPlus, One Checkerboard Square, St. Louis, MO 63164.

EXAMPLE 42

BUSINESS

Background. *School Foodservice & Nutrition* carried these full-page, color advertisements. Geared for the school food service professional, this magazine deals with school food service marketing and the needs of that industry. Included are items on nutrition, management, product advances, problems facing the industry, and trends in food. Which advertisement do you think was scored higher by Readex?

STUDENT ANALYSIS

NAME _____ CLASS _____ DATE _____

128

EXAMPLE 43

A

It's been one first after another ever since 1754. Devoe has been America's first choice of painters since before the Revolution, before the Constitution—even before America was America.

America's First. The Product, The Merchandising, The Marketing.

Now, during our 240th anniversary, we're looking for new dealers to help us grow and who want to grow with us. Here's what you've got going for you with Devoe. There are new Incentives and promotional programs. Plus there are innovative store designs and marketing support. And you've got one of the most comprehensive lines of top-quality paints and coatings for consumers and professionals—in the industry!

America's First. Advanced Coating Products Mean New Selling Opportunities.

Devoe has continued to advance paint research by developing new technology, waterborne, VOC-compliant paints as counterparts to the traditional solvent-based products. An example is Woodworks™, our newest line of waterborne interior wood finishing products.

Maybe It's Time For A Little Revolution Of Your Own.

If you're ready to increase your profitability, start by putting Devoe's 240 years of experience to work for you. Call us at 1-800-654-2616 and find out all the reasons why it pays to be a Devoe dealer.

B

If you're thinking about opening your own paint dealership, you'll want to brush up on Devoe's dealership program, because no paint company can help you open your door faster and easier than we can.

Go with Devoe, and you'll find yourself the owner of a total turn-key store that's ready for business. And you'll receive expert, comprehensive assistance with every decision you have to make, from store design to your grand opening promotions.

Devoe Puts You In Business.

Go with Devoe, and we'll furnish you with a complete stock of quality paints and sundries. And you won't pay one penny of interest on any of it for up to three years. With that kind of financial assistance, you can devote all your efforts to running your business.

But that's not the only reason to go with Devoe. Because we can also provide you with:

A Complete Product Line. Your store will feature a complete line of paints, innovative Devoe Coatings industrial products, stains, sundries, and more. You'll target every segment of the professional and do-it-yourself markets.

Proven Store Design. Our proven, consumer-friendly store design makes it easy for your customers to find what they need. People will want to come in to your store.

Co-op Advertising Dollars. Make your presence known with our marketing assistance. Use our co-op dollars to stretch your advertising budget.

Environmentally Friendly Products. Devoe is becoming the leader in waterborne coatings technology. You'll be able to supply products people feel good about using.

If you're ready to paint yourself a success, the right choice is Devoe's Dealer's Choice program. Find out more right now by calling 1-800-654-2616 toll free. In Kentucky call collect 1-502-897-9861. Your inquiry will be held in the strictest confidence.

EXAMPLE 43

BUSINESS

Background. Not surprisingly, these full-page advertisements appearing in *The Paint Dealer* were in full color. This publication is edited for the retail merchants of paint and associated sundries, such as paint stores, decorating centers, hardware and home center outlets, mass merchandisers, and discount department stores. It presents articles on product innovations, merchandising ideas, store management, news about paint, solvents, specialty coatings, adhesives, tools, applicators, and other paint-related products. Which advertisement do you think was scored higher by Readex?

STUDENT ANALYSIS

NAME _____ CLASS _____ DATE _____

EXAMPLE **44**

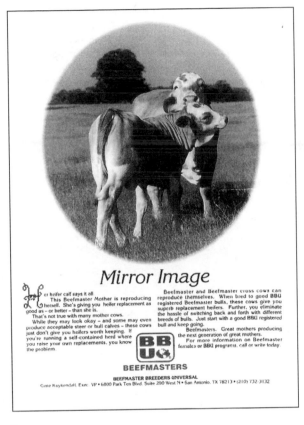

A

Her heifer calf says it all.

This Beefmaster Mother is reproducing herself. She's giving you heifer replacement as good as—or better—than she is.

That's not true with many mother cows.

While they may look okay—and some may even produce acceptable steer or bull calves—these cows just don't give you heifers worth keeping. If you're running a self-contained herd where you raise your own replacements, you know the problem.

Beefmaster and Beefmaster cross cows can reproduce themselves. When bred to good BBU registered Beefmaster bulls, these cows give you superb replacement heifers. Further, you eliminate the hassle of switching back and forth with different breeds of bulls. Just start with a good BBU registered bull and keep going.

Beefmasters. Great mothers producing the next generation of great mothers.

For more information on Beefmaster females or BBU programs, call or write today.

B

Jed Dillard, cattle manager for F.A. Boyd and Sons in the Florida Panhandle, started using high performing BBU registered Beefmaster bulls on his commercial cows eight years ago. Since then, he has increased weaning weights by 134 pounds, put some outstanding replacement females in the herd, enrolled most of his cows in BBU's Upgrading Program and is developing a strong market for the Beefmaster cross heifers. Write or call for his complete story.

Beefmasters. We're building for the next generation.

EXAMPLE **44**

BUSINESS

Background.   These full-page, full-color advertisements ran in *Progressive Farmer*, which concentrates its editorial content on the South and Southwest regions of the United States. Over 90 percent of the editorial content in *Progressive Farmer* is devoted to farm production and management, machinery, crops, livestock, and information applicable to southern agriculture. Which advertisement do you think was scored higher by Readex?

STUDENT ANALYSIS

NAME _____ CLASS _____ DATE _____

EXAMPLE 45

A

Big chunks of extra lean chicken make McDonald's® Chunky Chicken salad taste so good. You'll never guess it's low in fat, too. Only 6 grams with Lite Vinaigrette Dressing. And McDonald's Menu of the '90s offers your patients lots of choices like the 91% fat-free McLean Deluxe™ sandwich, freshly-tossed salads with reduced-calorie dressings, 1% lowfat mild and lowfat frozen yogurt.

McDonald's commitment to nutrition goes beyond our menu. We also offer an educational library including McDonald's Today. This brochure provides a nutrition analysis plus meal combinations like the one below with less than 30% of calories from fat. McDonald's wallet-sized Food Exchange List or Calorie, Fat, Cholesterol, and Sodium cards will help your patients meet their dietary needs.

For free samples of these materials or for more nutrition information about our menu, call 1-800-524-5900.

B

Times are changing and so is McDonald's®. Our Menu of the '90s continues to demonstrate our commitment to making responsible menu changes as lifestyles have changed and new technologies have developed. At the same time, our menu enhancements build on our tradition of offering top-quality food that tastes good. We've revolutionized the food industry with out 91% fat-free McLean Deluxe™ beef patty. We've cut saturated fat by 45% and eliminated cholesterol in our french fries by switching to 100% vegetable oil—the only oil we use. Our milk shakes are now 99.5% fat-free, and we've switched to lowfat frozen yogurt. We offer freshly-tossed salads with reduced-calorie dressings, and whole-grain cereals with 1% lowfat milk, so your patients can enjoy a variety of menu selections at McDonald's that fit within current dietary guidelines, like the combination shown here.

For health care professionals, we've developed new materials like "McDonald's Today™"—a brochure with a nutrition analysis of our menu and several meal combinations that fit within current dietary guidelines, and "What's Your Nutrition I.Q.?"—a fun quiz for patients developed with the National Center for Nutrition and Dietetics. For free samples of these materials for your patients and to learn more about McDonald's nutrition initiatives, call 1-800-524-5900.

EXAMPLE 45

BUSINESS

Background. These full-page, color advertisements ran in the *Journal of the American Dietetic Association*, which is edited for dietitians and nutritionists. Its content concentrates on managerial and professional personnel in food service and public health. Which advertisement do you think was scored higher by Readex?

STUDENT ANALYSIS

NAME _____ CLASS _____ DATE _____

EXAMPLE 46

A

Falcon Systems stocks, and in most cases can deliver in just 24 hours:

Product Line: System Memory, Internal Disk and Tape Devices, Striped Fast & Wide Disk Arrays (30 MB/sec.), FalconRAID arrays (Level 0, 3 and 5), Optical and Tape Libraries.

Falcon's products support a variety of systems, including:

Systems: Indy, Indigo/Indigo^2, Personal Iris, Professional Series, Power Series/Crimson, Challenge/Onyx

New Products: Falcon is also a leader in the development of products such as the FalconFLYTE Mounting System, which allows for the internal installation of disk, tape and optical devices on the Challenge/Onyx series. This exclusive Falcon product supports both Fast Single-ended and Fast/Wide Differential disk drives and eliminates the previous requirement of purchasing an 8-bit or 16-bit mounting SLED from SGI.

Warranties: Falcon's standard warrant is Five years for SCSI disk drives, Lifetime for memory products, and One and Two years for tape and optical devices. All warranties include a 24-hour Advanced Replacement Program, and all products qualify for the exclusive FalconCARE Extended Warranty Program.

B

Silicon Graphics created the challenge.

Falcon met it.

Four times the capacity.
Half the price.
Exclusively Falcon.

Follow your instincts.
Call for the new catalogue.

EXAMPLE 46

EXAMPLE 46

BUSINESS

Background. These full-page, full-color advertisements ran in *Computer Graphics World*, a magazine that covers the technologies of modeling, animation, and multimedia. These applications are divided among three key areas: engineering and science, art and entertainment, and presentation and training. Coverage focuses on the primary areas of graphics involvement with computers, computer-aided design and engineering for electronic and mechanical applications, and business and presentation graphics for architecture, engineering, and construction. Which advertisement do you think was scored higher by Readex?

STUDENT ANALYSIS

NAME _____ CLASS _____ DATE _____

EXAMPLE **47**

A

B

Fleet Manager for marine engine manufacturer Mercury Marine, Tom Scherg is proud of the three Cat 3406Bs in his fleet that have gone over one million miles without an engine overhaul. A good 95% of those miles are *loaded* miles. And 100% are run with Shell ROTELLA® T Multigrade with XLA™.

When we opened up one of these engines, the bright yellow paint on the crankcases internal surface was there for all to see. Very light deposits on the piston lands and ring grooves looked as if the engine had maybe 350,000 miles. The turbocharger hadn't even been rebuilt—it was the original!

Proven deposit control for more than a million miles without an overhaul—that's ROTELLA T with XLA.

''Our drivers are well-trained,'' Scherg says, ''And we use the best oil on the market. Frankly, I can't afford anything less.''

To find the Shell Jobber nearest you, look in the Yellow Pages under ''Oils—Lubricating'' or call 1-800-231-6950. And don't take our word for it that you'll get farther down the road with Shell RO-TELLA. Ask Tom Scherg.

Twenty-four-hour-a-day turnarounds—one driver by day and another by night—are a real stress test for any engine. But even though Standard Forwarding's 1984 Mack E6-300 had more than a million miles under its rings without an overhaul, it looked half its age when we tore it down.

Not a single broken or stuck ring. *Original* bearings still serviceable. Lots of crosshatch still visible on cylinder liners.

Bob Jurgensen is a Standard Forwarding driver who's also been director of fleet maintenance (that's him on the left). He gives credit to the company's dedicated drivers and mechanics. And to the only oil their engines ever see: ROTELLA® T Multigrade with XLA™.

For the Shell Jobber nearest you, look in the Yellow Pages under ''Oils—Lubricating'' or call 1-800-231-6950.

EXAMPLE 47

BUSINESS

Background. *Fleet Owner*, in which these full-page, color advertisements ran, is edited for management personnel responsible for purchasing, operating, and maintaining vehicles and equipment in truck and bus fleets having five or more vehicles. Articles cover management procedures, operating techniques, equipment and maintenance planning and practice, safety regulations, and prospective equipment developments. Which advertisement do you think was scored higher by Readex?

STUDENT ANALYSIS

NAME _____ CLASS _____ DATE _____

EXAMPLE **48**

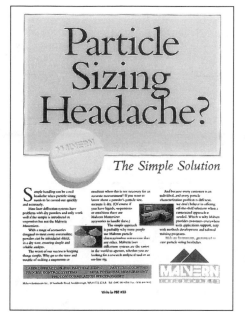

A

The Simple Solution

Sample handling can be a real headache when particle sizing needs to be carried out quickly and accurately.

Most laser diffraction systems have problems with dry powders and only work well if the sample is introduced in suspension but not the Malvern Mastersizer.

With a range of accessories designed to meet every eventuality; powders can be introduced direct, in a dry state, ensuring simple and reliable analysis.

The secret of our success is keeping things simple. Why go to the time and trouble of making a suspension or emulsion when this is not necessary for an accurate measurement? If you want to know about a powder's particle size, measure it dry. (Of course, if you have liquids, suspensions, or emulsions there are Malvern Mastersizer accessories to handle these.)

The simple approach is probably why more people use Malvern particle characterization instruments than any other. Malvern laser diffraction systems are the easiest in the world to operate, whether you are looking for a research analytical took or an on-line rig.

And because every customer is an individual, and every particle characterization problem is different, we don't believe in offering off-the-shelf solutions when a customized approach is needed. Which is why Malvern provides customers everywhere with applications support, help with methods development, and tailored training programs.

Malvern instruments, guaranteed to cure particle sizing headaches.

B

The bridge and the bloodsucker.

On the face of it, a bridge doesn't have a lot in common with a mosquito. Yet both are affected by Malvern's expertise in particle characterization.

Take the bridge. Like a chain, it is only as strong as its weakest link. In this case, the particles that make up the cement. So our instruments help measure and monitor the consistency of particle size to ensure that the strength of the resultant mix is not compromised.

The mosquito is more adversely affected—thanks to our instrument monitoring the particle size of the compound that makes up mosquito coils.

That's bad news for mosquitoes—good news for everyone else.

As world leaders in particle characterization, Malvern manufactures a range of instruments that ensure accurate and reliable data. Not just dry power samplers for cement or mosquito coils, but on-line systems as well as rigs for liquids and parenteral fluids. And not just for industry either, but also for research, quality control, laboratory and development applications.

Malvern also supply customized software, zeta potential instruments plus the world's most advanced photon correlation spectroscopy instrument. And we are on hand in over 50 countries around the world to offer support when and where you need it.

With Malvern, solutions also come in all shapes and sizes.

EXAMPLE 48

BUSINESS

Background. *Powder and Bulk Engineering* was the choice for these full-page, color advertisements. This magazine is edited for engineers and other technical managers in every processing industry segment where significant amounts of dry particulates are processed, handled, packaged, or stored. Which advertisement do you think was scored higher by Readex?

STUDENT ANALYSIS

NAME _____ CLASS _____ DATE _____

EXAMPLE 49

A

Parker controls keep food refrigerated before it gets to the supermarket.

Now supermarkets can bag the same advantages.

Nine out of 10 food processing and distribution plants depend on Parker controls to refrigerate their products under exacting temperature and humidity requirements.

Now supermarkets can enjoy the same efficiency and reliability. Because now Parker has a complete family of precise refrigeration controls designed to meet your specific needs.

For the machine room, we have our new widely acclaimed (S)PORT evaporator pressure regulator valves, which eliminate 4-flare connections, as well as our differentials and outlet regulators. Also our famous

Jackes-Evans solenoid valves, a full selection of TXVs, plus replaceable core dryers, sight glasses, and more.

For the walk-in freezer, a complete line of steel dryers, solenoid valves, and TXVs, featuring balanced port construction, that are all compatible with the new refrigerants.

For self-contained or remote display cases, TXVs for low, medium, and high temperature applications, plus a full range of our filters, regulators, solenoid valves, dryers, sight glasses, and check valves.

In addition to a supermarket-full of performance advantages, these Parker products also feature ease of installation and retrofit replacement.

Easy servicing, too. Call or write for our catalogue.

B

92% of food processing and distribution plants refrigerate with Parker controls.

Now the door is open to supermarkets.

Introducing a new, high efficiency evaporator pressure regulator valve for supermarket refrigeration.

More than 9 out of 10 food processing and distribution plants trust us to help keep their products at required temperatures.

So it makes sense for us to provide the same kind of reliable, efficient refrigeration after their products reach the supermarket.

We have everything it takes. With our new pressure regulator valve, Parker now offers a complete selection of controls for supermarket refrigerant management.

It's called the (S)PORT. Developed by our Refrigerating Specialties Division, it is the first inlet pressure regulator that requires no flare connections. This virtually eliminates all potential leaks.

This valve also uses low side inlet pressure

to open and close. Result: more exact inlet pressure control and increased system efficiency.

Competitive valves, on the other hand, require a high side header line to operate their valves. Besides being less precise, this increases installation costs and decreases system efficiency.

The (S)PORT is also the first valve of its kind with a replaceable cartridge that lets you change capacities—without removing the valve. The valve itself comes in 5 port sizes, from 3/8'' to 1-3/8'', and 5 connection sizes from 7/8'' to 2-1/8'', so you can better match your system requirements in the field.

The unique (S)PORT joins a proven group of controls available for supermarket refrigeration under the Parker banner. It includes our famous Jackes-Evans solenoid valves as well as our popular Parker line of thermostatic expansion valves, in all required sizes.

Do what the food processing plants do. Insist on Parker. Call or write for our catalog.

EXAMPLE 49

BUSINESS

Background. These full-page, full-color advertisements ran in *The News: Airconditioning, Heating & Refrigeration News*. This publication focuses on industry news and informational features on topics for hvac/r contractors, wholesalers, manufacturers, distributors, and engineers. Editorial content covers technical, marketing, design, engineering, installation, management, and labor areas. Which advertisement do you think was scored higher by Readex?

STUDENT ANALYSIS

NAME _____ CLASS _____ DATE _____

EXAMPLE **50**

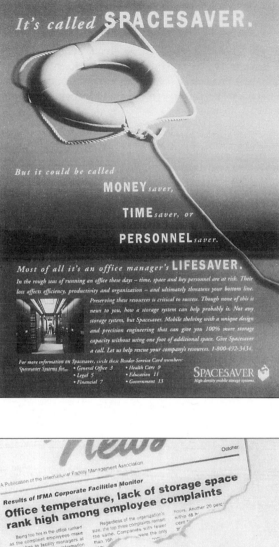

A

It's called Spacesaver. But it could be called Moneysaver, Time-saver, or Personnelsaver.

Most of all it's an office manager's Lifesaver.

In the rough seas of running an office these days—time, space, and key personnel are at risk. Their loss affects efficiency, productivity and organization—and ultimately threatens your bottom line. Preserving these resources is critical to success. Though none of this is news to you, how a storage system can help probably is. Not any storage system, but Spacesaver. Mobile shelving with a unique design and precision engineering that can give you 100% more storage capacity without using one foot of additional space. Give Spacesaver a call. Let us help rescue your company's resources. 1-800-492-3434.

B

Being too hot or too cold isn't cool at all. The second hottest issue is a lack of storage space. "Where do I put all this stuff?" rings through offices nationwide. There is one company that's listening. Spacesaver, the premier manufacturer of mobile store systems—mobile shelving with a unique design and precision engineering that can give you 100% more storage capacity in the same space. That not only helps cool down tempers, that's good business. Spacesaver increases work efficiency and productivity, and it does it in space that used to be wasted. Give Spacesaver a call. We'll show you some pretty cool ideas. 1-800-492-3434.

EXAMPLE 50

BUSINESS

Background. *Architecture* magazine was the choice for these full-color, full-page advertisements. This publication is edited for architects, specifiers, and design professionals responsible for designing and specifying today's new building construction, existing rehabilitation, and remodeling projects. Editorial content focuses on analytical evaluation of new and existing buildings, news that affects the profession, new products, government, and management-related articles. Which advertisement do you think was scored higher by Readex?

STUDENT ANALYSIS

NAME _____ CLASS _____ DATE _____